Privacy Preserving Data Mining for Online Social Networks

BY

Rodrigo

TABLE OF CONTENTS

CHAPTER-I
INTRODUCTION

1.1. Introduction

Online Social Media (OSM) platforms have become an integral part of everyday communication and information sharing [1]. From connecting with family and friends to voicing opinions on public issues, these platforms support a wide range of social interactions. With the rise of digital connectivity, people now share large volumes of personal, professional and location-specific data through posts, messages, multimedia content and network connections [2]. However, this open exchange of information raises significant concerns about privacy, data protection and misuse of personal content. As digital footprints expand, the risks associated with unauthorized data access, identity theft, misinformation and social profiling have grown considerably. Personal information once considered private is now often exposed intentionally or unintentionally on public or semi-public networks. This exposure enables third parties, including advertisers, data brokers and malicious entities, to track, analyse and exploit user behaviour. Consequently, users may face targeted manipulation, reputation damage, or privacy violations without their knowledge or consent. The fundamental problem lies in the imbalance between data sharing and data protection. While users are encouraged to engage freely and often unknowingly grant extensive permissions to platforms, the tools available to manage privacy are often inadequate, overly complex, or difficult to configure. Additionally, current security measures typically focus on technical vulnerabilities rather than behavioural patterns and contextual threats. As a result, individuals are left vulnerable to emerging threats that go beyond simple data breaches.

The challenge is further complicated by the dynamic nature of online social interactions. Unlike static datasets, OSM content is generated in real time, shared across networks and influenced by the actions of other users [3]. A user's privacy can be compromised not only by their own actions but also by the content or behaviour of their connections. This interconnected environment calls for adaptive, context-aware privacy solutions that extend beyond conventional access control and data anonymization. The increasing volume and complexity of online interactions demand robust frameworks that preserve user privacy while enabling secure communication and data usage. Effective privacy preservation should not hinder platform functionality or user experience. Instead, it must operate in the background, enforcing policies and protecting sensitive data without compromising the interactive nature of social media.

This research addresses the critical need for privacy preservation in OSM by investigating methods that analyse user behaviour, control data access based on policy and detect potential threats with high accuracy. The study focuses on creating a structured, multi-layered approach that considers user intentions, relationship contexts and data sensitivity. By integrating analytical techniques, encryption mechanisms and classification models, the research aims to develop a comprehensive solution that safeguards users from both internal and external privacy risks. The significance of this research lies in its ability to enhance trust in digital communication platforms. In an era where online presence is deeply intertwined with personal identity, protecting that presence becomes essential. Ensuring that users can engage without fear of exploitation contributes to a safer, more ethical and more inclusive digital environment [4]. This chapter introduces the research problem, outlines the objectives, defines the scope and highlights the motivation behind the study. It sets the stage for a detailed discussion of existing literature, methodological approaches, system design, experimental results and the overall contributions of the research presented in the chapters that follow.

1.2. Data Mining Techniques for Privacy Preservation

Data mining plays a vital role in extracting meaningful patterns, trends and insights from large datasets [5]. However, when dealing with personal or sensitive information especially in domains like online social media, healthcare and finance privacy becomes a significant concern.

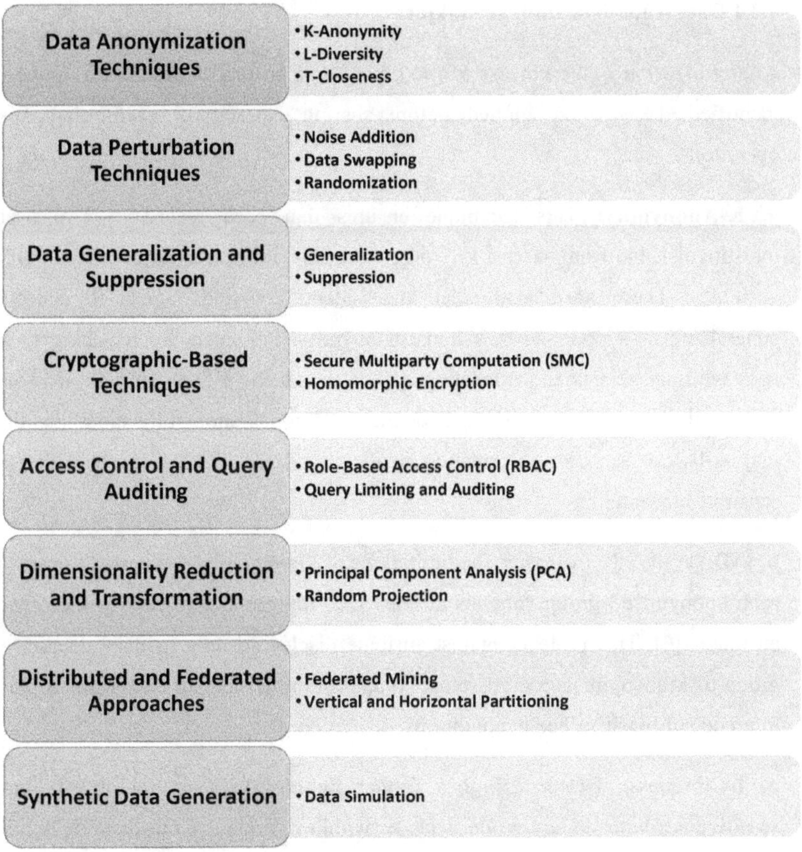

Figure 1.1 Data Mining Techniques for Privacy Preservation

Privacy-preserving data mining (PPDM) focuses on protecting individual privacy while still enabling useful data analysis. This field combines data transformation, access control, cryptographic methods and statistical modelling to ensure that personal identities and confidential data remain secure throughout the mining process [5]. Several techniques have emerged to address this challenge, balancing utility and privacy. These techniques can broadly be categorized into data anonymization, transformation, perturbation, access control and distributed learning models.

1.2.1 Data Anonymization Techniques

Anonymization is the process of modifying data so that individuals cannot be re-identified. It is often applied before sharing datasets or performing mining operations.

a. K-Anonymity: This technique ensures that each record in a dataset is indistinguishable from at least k−1 other records with respect to certain identifying attributes. These attributes, called quasi-identifiers (e.g., age, ZIP code), are generalized or suppressed to achieve anonymity. For example, replacing specific ages with age ranges and truncating ZIP codes can help form clusters of identical entries, thus protecting individual identities. While k-anonymity hides identity, it may still leak sensitive information if all individuals in a group share the same sensitive attribute.

b. L-Diversity: To overcome the limitations of k-anonymity, l-diversity ensures that each anonymized group contains at least well-represented values for the sensitive attributes [6]. This protects against attribute disclosure. In a medical dataset, each group of k-anonymous records must contain multiple distinct diagnoses to prevent inference of sensitive health conditions.

c. T-Closeness: T-closeness goes further by ensuring that the distribution of sensitive attributes in any group is close (within threshold 't') to the distribution of those attributes in the overall dataset. This minimizes the risk of inference attacks.

1.2.2. Data Perturbation Techniques

Perturbation modifies the data in such a way that the overall patterns are preserved for analysis, but individual data values are distorted.

a. Noise Addition: Random noise is added to numerical data, preserving aggregate statistics like mean and variance while concealing exact values. This is often used in privacy protection for income, medical, or browsing history datasets [7]. While it preserves utility to a certain extent, high noise levels can degrade mining accuracy.

b. Data Swapping: Values between records are exchanged to break the linkage between identity and sensitive data. This method keeps data distributions unchanged but complicates re-identification. Swapping the income field between two individuals of similar demographic profiles is an example for the problem.

c. Randomization: Data is distorted using controlled randomness, often in classification tasks. This approach helps mask individual data while still allowing general pattern recognition.

1.2.3. Data Generalization and Suppression

These techniques involve reducing data granularity to protect identities.

a. Generalization: Specific values are replaced by more general ones. For example, replacing "35 years" with "30–40 years" or "New York City" with "New York State."

b. Suppression: Data values or entire records are removed if they pose a high risk of identification. This method is particularly effective when few records are outliers or unique. For example, removing birthdate fields when only a few records have unique combinations of other attributes [8].

1.2.4. Cryptographic-Based Techniques

These techniques rely on secure computation and encryption protocols to perform data mining without exposing raw data.

a. Secure Multiparty Computation (SMC): SMC allows multiple parties to collaboratively compute a function over their inputs while keeping those inputs private. Each party only sees its own data and the final output. Banks computing fraud patterns collectively without sharing customer transaction data.

b. Homomorphic Encryption: This form of encryption allows computation directly on encrypted data. The result, when decrypted, matches the outcome as if it had been performed on unencrypted data. This technique enables privacy-preserving data mining without decrypting sensitive data, although it can be computationally intensive.

1.2.5. Access Control and Query Auditing

Rather than modifying the data, this approach limits who can access the data and under what conditions.

a. Role-Based Access Control (RBAC): Access to data is restricted based on user roles (e.g., admin, analyst, guest). Sensitive data is only available to users with the appropriate clearance.

b. Query Limiting and Auditing: Systems monitor and limit the number of queries that can be executed, particularly those that attempt to extract identifying information. Suspicious access patterns are flagged and logged.

1.2.6. Dimensionality Reduction and Transformation: Reducing the number of features or transforming the data can also enhance privacy.

a. Principal Component Analysis (PCA): PCA reduces data dimensionality by projecting it onto orthogonal components that capture the most variance. This transforms data into a new space, reducing its interpretability and thus aiding privacy.

b. Random Projection: Another method of reducing dimensions by projecting data into a lower-dimensional space using random matrices. This preserves distance metrics approximately while reducing data sensitivity.

1.2.7. Distributed and Federated Approaches

Instead of aggregating data at a central location, computations are distributed across local sources, reducing the risk of exposing sensitive information.

a. Federated Mining: Data remains at the local devices and only model updates are shared. This ensures that raw data never leaves its source.

b. Vertical and Horizontal Partitioning: In vertically partitioned data, different attributes are stored at different locations. In horizontal partitioning, different records are split across sources. Mining is done collaboratively without pooling raw data.

1.2.8. Synthetic Data Generation

Instead of using original datasets, synthetic datasets are generated that resemble real data in terms of structure and distribution but contain no actual records.

a. **Data Simulation:** Synthetic records are created based on patterns in the original data, preserving statistical properties while ensuring no individual's data is exposed [9]. Generating health records that mirror trends in hospital data without referencing any real patient is an example for the simulation of data.

Privacy preservation in data mining requires a careful balance between data utility and individual confidentiality. Techniques such as k-anonymity, data perturbation, encryption and access control are instrumental in building systems that are both secure and analytically useful. Each method comes with trade-offs and often, multiple techniques are combined to meet specific privacy goals. As data continues to grow in both volume and sensitivity, the demand for privacy-preserving solutions becomes increasingly important. Effective data mining must not only discover useful knowledge but also respect the rights and privacy of the individuals behind the data.

1.3. Privacy Preservation in Online Social Media – Background Study

Online Social Media (OSM) platforms have become indispensable to modern life, serving as virtual spaces for communication, collaboration, content sharing and public discourse. With billions of users actively engaged on platforms such as Facebook, Twitter, Instagram and LinkedIn, these services host vast amounts of personal, behavioural and relational data. While these platforms offer convenience and connectivity, they also introduce serious privacy challenges. Users often share personal information with varying levels of sensitivity ranging from names and locations to political views, photographs and health-related updates. Without proper safeguards, this information can be exploited by unauthorized entities for surveillance, profiling, phishing and other harmful purposes. This background study explores the landscape of privacy concerns in online social media, historical developments, key risks and the evolution of methods designed to preserve user privacy while maintaining functionality and usability.

1.3.1. Evolution of Online Social Media and Its Impact on Privacy

Online social platforms initially emerged as tools for academic networking and community sharing, but quickly evolved into global systems for real-time communication and digital identity representation. The social graph a model representing user relationships became central to content recommendation, advertising targeting and information dissemination. As these platforms gained popularity, they began collecting extensive personal and interactional data [10]. Early models lacked strong privacy controls, allowing user profiles, friend lists and activities to be publicly accessible by default. Over time, users and regulators raised concerns about misuse of personal data, leading to the gradual introduction of privacy settings and user consent models. However, despite these improvements, privacy breaches remained frequent. Incidents involving unauthorized data harvesting, location tracking, account takeovers and targeted disinformation campaigns highlighted the vulnerabilities of centralized and loosely regulated social platforms.

1.3.2. Key Privacy Risks in Online Social Media

There are few risks identified in the OSM that prevents the research in a complete manner. They are enumerated below:

a. Identity Exposure: Users often reveal identifying details such as full names, birthdays, school affiliations and employment history. When combined with posts, likes and tags, these details can be used to reconstruct user identities, even when profile information is partially hidden.

b. Inference Attacks: Even if direct identifiers are removed, attackers can use patterns in user behaviour, social connections and language usage to infer sensitive attributes. For example, political beliefs, religious affiliations and health conditions can often be deduced from post content and group memberships.

c. Data Mining and Profiling: Third parties including marketers and malicious actors exploit public or semi-public data for profiling. This data can be used to manipulate user behaviours, target vulnerable individuals, or conduct discriminatory filtering, especially in job recruitment, lending, or insurance.

d. Location and Context Leakage: Many users unknowingly share location data through photos, check-ins, or metadata. This can lead to physical stalking, unauthorized surveillance, or theft when location patterns are publicly accessible.

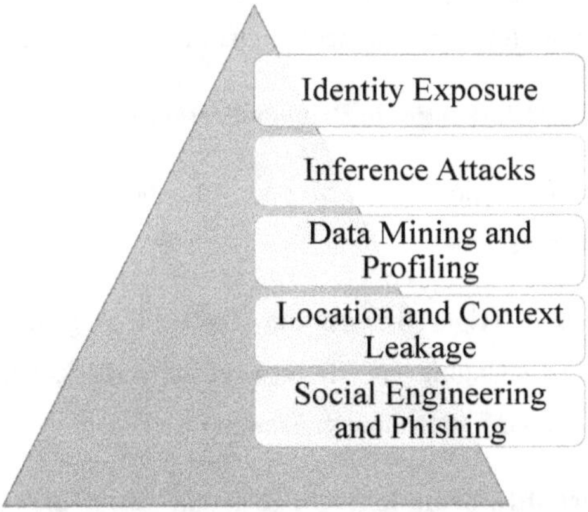

Figure 1.2 Privacy Risks in Online Social Media (OSM)

e. Social Engineering and Phishing: Attackers often gather background information from social media to craft personalized phishing messages. This tactic is highly effective as it mimics legitimate communication, making users more likely to reveal passwords or financial data.

1.3.3. Regulatory Framework and Policy Responses

In response to growing concerns, several regulatory initiatives have been introduced to address privacy protection:

- **General Data Protection Regulation (GDPR)**: Enforced in the European Union since 2018, GDPR mandates explicit consent for data processing, the right to be forgotten, data portability and transparency in data handling.
- **California Consumer Privacy Act (CCPA)**: Provides users with rights to know what data is collected, request its deletion and opt out of data sales.

- **Platform-Specific Policies**: Major social networks have introduced privacy dashboards, visibility settings and data download options. However, enforcement remains inconsistent and complex interfaces often discourage users from managing their privacy settings effectively [11].

While these regulations represent progress, they are not universally applicable and enforcement varies across jurisdictions. Moreover, compliance depends heavily on user awareness and the willingness of platforms to act transparently.

1.3.4. Technical Challenges in Privacy Preservation

Privacy protection in OSM poses unique challenges not encountered in traditional databases:

a. Dynamic and High-Dimensional Data: User-generated content is often unstructured, fast-changing and diverse. Posts, images, reactions and friendships evolve rapidly, making static anonymization insufficient.

b. Interconnected Information: The relational nature of social media complicates privacy preservation. A user's data may be exposed not only through their actions but also through posts or tags made by others in their network.

c. User-Driven Content Control: Unlike structured datasets managed by organizations, social media data is generated by users. This makes centralized privacy enforcement difficult, as content boundaries often blur across users, groups and public pages.

d. Utility-Privacy Trade-Off: Effective privacy protection often reduces data utility. Excessive anonymization or restriction can degrade platform functionality, affecting personalization, recommendations and social discovery.

1.3.5. Existing Techniques for Privacy Protection in Social Media

Several strategies have been proposed to preserve privacy in social platforms:

a. Anonymization and Obfuscation: Early techniques focused on removing identifiers or generalizing sensitive attributes. While useful, these methods are prone to re-identification attacks through correlation with external datasets.

b. Access Control and Visibility Settings: Platforms allow users to define who can view their posts, profiles and activity. While necessary, these settings are often confusing or too simplistic, leading to unintentional exposure.

c. Encryption-Based Protection: Attribute-based encryption allows users to share content securely with selected groups based on attribute rules (e.g., "friends in school group"). This ensures that even the platform cannot access the raw content.

d. Privacy-Aware Recommendation Systems: Instead of using complete user profiles, privacy-aware systems generate recommendations using partial or obfuscated data [12]. This balances personalization with privacy.

e. Differential Privacy: This technique introduces statistical noise to query outputs, making it difficult to link results back to individual users. Although more common in centralized databases, it is gaining attention in social media analytics.

1.3.6. Recent Research Trends and Gaps

Recent academic work has expanded privacy preservation techniques in areas such as behavioural modelling, trust evaluation and dynamic access control. Multi-layered frameworks have been proposed that combine threat detection, policy enforcement and encryption to protect users throughout their interaction cycle. However, key challenges remain:

- **Scalability**: Many advanced techniques struggle with performance at the scale of modern social networks.
- **Real-Time Implementation**: Methods like graph-based access control and kernelized evaluation are computationally intensive and difficult to apply in real-time.
- **User Awareness**: Despite technical tools, privacy still depends heavily on user behaviours and understanding.

There is also a growing interest in integrating contextual information such as interaction frequency, topic relevance and content sensitivity to fine-tune privacy levels dynamically. Privacy preservation in online social media is a multidimensional problem that spans technical, behavioural and regulatory domains[13]. The complexity of social interactions, coupled with the richness of user-generated content, requires solutions that go beyond simple access control or data masking. A well-rounded privacy framework must include threat detection, trust analysis, encrypted data sharing and dynamic policy enforcement, all while maintaining usability and platform responsiveness. The study of privacy in online social platforms continues to evolve and future systems must integrate technical innovation with user education and transparent governance to ensure that privacy becomes a fundamental feature rather than a secondary concern.

1.4. Research Problem

Online Social Media (OSM) platforms have transformed global communication by enabling rapid content sharing, relationship building and real-time interaction. However, this convenience comes at the cost of user privacy, data misuse and malicious behaviours proliferation. With the increasing reliance on cloud infrastructure and the unregulated exchange of personal information, users are frequently exposed to content manipulation, identity theft and unauthorized access to their private data.

Traditional security mechanisms are largely reactive, failing to proactively evaluate user credibility or ensure data privacy at a granular level. Additionally, most threat detection systems lack integration with privacy-preserving models, leading to either overexposure of user data or underperformance in identifying high-risk entities. Thus, there is an urgent need for a unified, layered framework that addresses user trust, access regulation and threat evaluation while upholding individual privacy across all levels of interaction.

The core research problem can be stated as:

"How can privacy preservation be systematically enforced in Online Social Media environments while ensuring accurate threat detection, secure data access and minimal exposure of user-sensitive information?"

This problem requires addressing three interconnected challenges:

- **Trust and behaviours assessment:** How to identify and monitor potentially harmful users without breaching privacy?

- **Access control and data confidentiality:** How to regulate who accesses what information and under what conditions?

- **Accurate threat evaluation:** How to detect malicious entities with high precision while maintaining data utility?

These challenges are tackled through a multi-phase framework in this research with techniques from Data Mining and Machine Learning Techniques.

1.4.1. Trust-Based User Scoring

Let each user be represented by a vector of behavioural and profile attributes [14] as given in Eq.1.1.

$$\boldsymbol{U_i = \{a1, a2, \ldots, an\}} \qquad \textbf{Eq.1.1.}$$

Where each 'aj' denotes parameters such as profile consistency, interaction integrity, prior violations and credibility of shared content [15]. A Trust Score Ti is calculated as given in Eq.1.2.

$$\boldsymbol{T_i = \sum_{j=1}^{n} w_i \cdot a_i} \qquad \textbf{Eq.1.2.}$$

Where $\boldsymbol{w_i}$ represents the weight assigned to attribute $\boldsymbol{a_i}$. This score is dynamic and updated with each user activity. Users are classified based on the following thresholds:

- Ti>80: Trusted
- 60≤Ti≤80: Moderately Trusted
- 40≤Ti<60: Neutral
- Ti<40: Suspicious

This computation enables proactive detection of unusual behaviours while protecting benign users from undue restrictions.

1.4.2. Access Regulation via Attribute Matching

Let $D_k = ID_k, C_k$ represent data entries contributed by users, where C_k is a set of credential attributes [16]. Each data record is assigned a Privacy Level P_k from {Low, Medium, High} based on a function $f(C_k)$.

An access request$R_u = SK_u, A_u$, where SK_u is the user's secret key and A_u is the set of attributes, is evaluated for permission as given in Eq.1.3.

$$\boldsymbol{Grant(R_k, D_k)} = \begin{cases} \boldsymbol{1, if\ SK_u\ is\ valid\ and} \quad \boldsymbol{A_u \sqsupseteq Policy_k} \\ \boldsymbol{0, Otherwise} \end{cases} \quad \textbf{Eq.1.3.}$$

Only when the request is valid and the attributes match the required policy is the decryption key issued for that data. This approach ensures attribute-level access control, minimizing overexposure of sensitive data. In addition, flow-graph validation is performed using Eq.1.4.

$$\boldsymbol{FG = (N, E, \varphi)} \quad \textbf{Eq.1.4}$$

Where N represents the Set of users, E the Directed trust-based edges and φ the Flow parameters (confidence, coverage, trust) respectively. A request is granted only if a valid path with sufficient φ exists between requester and data owner.

1.4.3. Ensemble Threat Detection

The final phase introduces a composite evaluation strategy integrating clustering, tree-based classification and high-dimensional similarity analysis.

Let Xi denote the feature vector of user iii, composed of numerical and categorical attributes extracted from user behaviours.

- **Clustering:** Users are grouped using distance $d(X_i, X_j)$, where d is a suitable metric (e.g., Euclidean).
- **Classification:** A decision tree model T(X) outputs a label Li based on feature splits.
- **Kernelized Similarity:** Features are projected into higher dimensions using transformation $\boldsymbol{\varphi}$ (X) and similarity is evaluated using composite metrics.

A final user classification Ci is determined as given in Eq.1.5.

$$\boldsymbol{C_i} = \begin{cases} \boldsymbol{Malicious, if\ flagged\ by\ IDS, DT\ and\ KNN} \\ \boldsymbol{Normal, Otherwise} \end{cases} \quad \textbf{Eq.1.5.}$$

This consensus-based evaluation significantly reduces false positives while maintaining precision.

1.5. Objective of the Research

The overarching goal of this research is to design a layered, privacy-preserving framework for Online Social Media (OSM) that facilitates early threat detection, secure data access and adaptive user classification while ensuring minimal exposure of private information.

This objective is addressed through three specific objectives of phases as given below:

- **TRIDENT**: Establishing a secure trust scoring mechanism that profiles users based on behavioural analysis and content integrity.
- **PRIVAFLOW**: Enforcing attribute-level access control using encrypted credentials and relationship validation to safeguard data privacy.
- **DEEP-SECURE**: Delivering high-accuracy user classification and malicious behaviours detection through ensemble learning and kernel-based similarity modelling.

Together, these modules offer a complete privacy preservation solution for OSNs starting from user evaluation to encrypted data access and concluding with deep threat analytics.

1.6. Overall framework of the Research

The research presents a multi-phase framework aimed at detecting threats, safeguarding user data and ensuring privacy within Online Social Networks (OSNs) called **Multi-Phase Secure and Privacy-Preserving System for Social Media Threat Handling (MSPPS-SMTH) Framework.** The design consists of three distinct but interconnected phases: (1) Trust-based behavioural assessment and threat detection, (2) Privacy-regulated data access and control and (3) High-accuracy ensemble evaluation and optimization. Each phase builds upon the previous, forming a comprehensive system that evolves from basic trust scoring to advanced detection and privacy enforcement. The overall architecture of the Framework is given in Figure 1.3

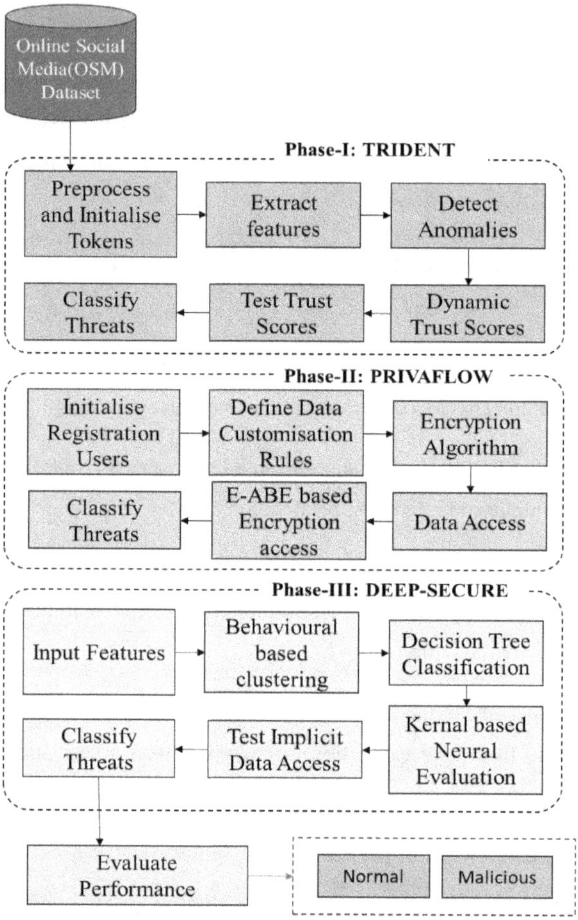

Figure 1.3 Multi-Phase Secure and Privacy-Preserving System for Social Media Threat Handling (MSPPS-SMTH) Framework.

Phase I: TRIDENT – Trust-Integrated Data Mining and Evaluation Network for Threat Handling

The first phase lays the foundation by focusing on identifying trust metrics and detecting malicious behaviours through structured data mining. This component, referred to as TRIDENT, introduces a secure interaction model that evaluates user authenticity, monitors behavioural patterns and classifies users based on trustworthiness.

Initially, social media users are registered and provided with Trust Initialization Tokens (TITs) containing profile information, verification status and prior behavioural data. These tokens form the basis for dynamic trust score computation. A Trust Evaluation Matrix is then used to assess profile consistency, integrity of interactions, credibility of mutual connections and the reliability of shared content. These trust scores are constantly updated to reflect changes in user behaviour.

Subsequently, behavioural profiling is implemented using frequent pattern mining and rule-based learning. This analysis captures key indicators such as post duplication, rapid link dissemination and abnormal interaction spikes to highlight suspicious activity. Simultaneously, content risk is evaluated using lexical and semantic techniques to detect misinformation, spam and harmful content.

To identify anomalies, user activities are grouped using a combination of density-based and centroid-based clustering. Outliers in these clusters are flagged for further scrutiny. A multi-layer classification system, combining decision tree logic with support vector analysis, categorizes users into benign, suspicious, or malicious.

Trust scores are adjusted based on feedback and system-detected violations. Users falling below specific thresholds face access limitations or temporary bans. This phase culminates in a data-centric engine, SOCMINE, which filters social media interactions and delivers labelled user classifications. It forms the primary line of defence by pre-emptively identifying and segregating potential threats.

Phase II: PRIVAFLOW – Privacy-Regulated Information Verification and Access Framework with FISARA

Building upon the classifications made in TRIDENT, the second phase, titled PRIVAFLOW, shifts focus toward secure and privacy-aware data management. This phase introduces a controlled access model to ensure that user data is shared and retrieved in a manner aligned with individual privacy policies and system-level rules.

All users and data owners undergo a structured registration process within a secure cloud environment. Data owners define the sensitivity of their information through customizable privacy rules. These rules are enforced during data submission, classifying the data into various confidentiality levels (low, medium, or high). Submitted data is then encrypted using an enhanced attribute-based encryption method (E-ABE), ensuring that only authorized users can access relevant data segments.

When a user initiates a request to access data, their secret key and associated attributes are validated against pre-defined policies. Unauthorized or mismatched access attempts are immediately blocked. Access rights are also contingent on flow-graph validation, where directed relationships between users are analysed. A user can access data only if a validated edge exists in the flow graph, indicating a secure, trusted and contextually valid connection with the data owner.

Further checks are performed through attribute policy matching. Only if the user's attributes satisfy all required conditions is a decryption key issued. Data matching both the request and the allowed attribute scope is then decrypted and made available. Additionally, compatibility between the user's privacy profile and the data's confidentiality level is assessed through a cost-privacy model, which filters out non-compliant services.

The final layer involves secure retrieval from the cloud storage, with comprehensive logging of all access activities. PRIVAFLOW ensures that data is protected from unauthorized disclosures while maintaining system usability. Its contribution lies in enforcing precise and adaptive privacy rules without compromising efficiency, forming a vital middle layer between detection and decision-making.

Phase III: DEEP-SECURE – Deep Ensemble Evaluation and Privacy System Using KENSURE

The final phase introduces an advanced, multi-layered evaluation system that synthesizes clustering, decision logic and kernel-based classification to refine user assessment and threat detection. Known as DEEP-SECURE, this phase addresses challenges related to false positives, classification accuracy and adaptive evaluation of evolving threat behaviours.

Initially, raw data collected from user activities including URL patterns, IP access history, binary behavioural flags and linguistic traits is normalized and vectorized. These features are used to segment users into behaviour-based clusters using an iterative distance-based algorithm. This clustering acts as the first line of anomaly detection by grouping users with similar activity profiles and highlighting outliers.

Next, a decision tree classifier, built using CART methodology, is trained on the clustered data. It uses attribute splitting based on statistical measures such as Gini index and entropy to assign labels malicious or normal. Overfitting is reduced through pruning techniques, which eliminate overly complex branches, thus enhancing classification robustness.

The third layer introduces a kernel-enhanced neural model that projects user data into a high-dimensional space, improving discrimination between subtle behavioural variations. It applies a combination of distance metrics including Euclidean, Hamming, Riemannian and Mahala Nobis to assess user similarity. Classification is finalized using a k-nearest neighbours voting strategy, assigning labels based on proximity within the transformed feature space.

An ensemble mechanism integrates the results of all three models—clustering, decision tree and kernel classifier. Only users flagged by all three are definitively marked as malicious. This consensus-based approach dramatically reduces false positives while maximizing detection accuracy. Confirmed threats are removed from the data pool, while trustworthy user data is retained for further system personalization and interaction refinement.

DEEP-SECURE, powered by the KENSURE algorithm, provides the highest level of threat evaluation in the framework. It balances robust security enforcement with system scalability and user content integrity.

This three-phase framework offers a structured and comprehensive solution to secure and manage online social interactions. TRIDENT initiates the process by evaluating trust and identifying threats. PRIVAFLOW follows with encrypted access control, ensuring privacy compliance. DEEP-SECURE concludes the process with high-accuracy classification, leveraging ensemble learning and advanced similarity modelling. Together, these phases form a cohesive pipeline that filters, protects and optimizes user data within social media ecosystems, ensuring both security and user privacy across all operational levels.

1.7. Contributions of the Research

This research introduces a comprehensive, multi-phase framework aimed at ensuring privacy preservation and secure data interaction in Online Social Media (OSM) environments. The primary contributions of this work span across trust-based evaluation, policy-regulated access control and advanced threat detection, offering a layered defence mechanism that integrates seamlessly with user-centric platforms [17]. Each phase of the framework addresses a unique challenge within the privacy-security domain and collectively provides a robust and scalable solution for modern social networks.

The first contribution lies in the design and implementation of a behaviour-based trust evaluation system that detects suspicious patterns among users. This component introduces dynamic trust scoring based on factors such as profile consistency, engagement integrity and interaction credibility. By incorporating frequent pattern mining and anomaly detection through hybrid clustering methods, the system classifies users into trustworthy, neutral, or malicious categories. This proactive filtering mechanism enables early threat identification and minimizes the spread of harmful content, impersonation, or manipulation on the platform.

The second major contribution is the creation of a privacy-regulated information sharing framework, which uses enhanced attribute-based encryption (E-

ABE) and flow-graph validation to enforce fine-grained access control. This model allows data owners to define personalized privacy rules, categorize data by sensitivity and control how their content is shared. Through secure key generation and attribute matching, the system ensures that only authorized users with valid credentials and verified trust relationships can access protected content. By combining privacy levels, flow-based validation and compatibility checks, this component prevents unauthorized data disclosure while preserving usability.

The third contribution involves the design of an ensemble evaluation system that enhances the accuracy of malicious user detection. This system integrates three distinct layers: a clustering-based intrusion detection system, a decision tree classifier and a kernelized neural evaluation model. By analysing user behaviour in high-dimensional spaces and applying majority consensus, the model significantly reduces false positives and enhances threat prediction accuracy. Users are only flagged as malicious when all three mechanisms independently identify them as such, ensuring high reliability and fairness.

An overarching contribution of this research is the unification of these three components TRIDENT, PRIVAFLOW and DEEP-SECURE into a single operational pipeline. The framework transitions from behavioural trust evaluation, to secure data handling and finally to advanced detection and classification. This layered structure not only improves security and privacy in isolation but also ensures holistic protection across the full data lifecycle. Collectively, these contributions address critical gaps in existing OSM security systems by providing a scalable, adaptable and privacy-preserving framework. The research lays the foundation for future developments in secure user interaction, encrypted content sharing and intelligent threat detection in decentralized and dynamic online environments.

1.8. Scope of the Research

This research focuses on developing a comprehensive, privacy-preserving framework for secure interaction, data sharing and threat detection in Online Social Media (OSM) environments. With the growing reliance on digital communication platforms and the increasing volume of personal information shared online, ensuring privacy and preventing misuse of user data have become pressing challenges [18]. The scope of this research is defined by the range of technical, functional and security aspects addressed through its three-phase design: behavioural trust analysis, privacy-enforced data access and advanced threat classification.

The study is centred on cloud-supported social media platforms where users generate a wide variety of content, including posts, messages, images and links. These platforms facilitate complex social interactions and store both structured and unstructured data. The research considers diverse user behaviours and real-time content exchange, focusing on the challenges of monitoring, evaluating and securing such data streams without compromising user experience or performance.

The scope includes the prevention of identity disclosure, unauthorized data access, behavioural profiling and information leakage. It also ensures secure data processing through encryption and policy enforcement mechanisms. The research supports privacy at multiple levels content, user relationships and access rights without sacrificing the usability or scalability of the platform.

The framework is designed to be adaptable to various social media platforms and scalable for large user bases. It supports both centralized and cloud-based environments, making it relevant for platforms that manage millions of daily interactions. The research also accommodates the possibility of integration with existing security models and compliance with privacy regulations such as GDPR and CCPA. In summary, the scope of this research covers the full spectrum of privacy and security challenges in online social media—from user behaviour assessment to secure content sharing and robust threat classification. It offers a holistic solution that aligns technical mechanisms with user privacy expectations, making it applicable to current and future digital communication platforms.

1.9. Social Significance of the Research

In the digital era, Online Social Media (OSM) platforms have become essential tools for communication, information exchange and public engagement. From sharing personal milestones to organizing social movements, individuals increasingly depend on these platforms for both private and public interaction.

However, this reliance comes with significant risks, particularly in terms of user privacy, data security and exposure to malicious activities [19]. The social significance of this research lies in its direct contribution to making digital interactions safer, more private and more trustworthy.

Privacy is a fundamental human right and its protection in online environments is vital. This research provides a structured approach to ensure that users retain control over their personal data. By incorporating attribute-based encryption, policy-based access control and trust evaluation, the framework allows users to determine who can access their content and under what conditions. This empowers individuals, particularly vulnerable groups such as minors, activists and marginalized communities, to engage online without fear of surveillance, exploitation, or misuse of their information.

One of the major challenges facing social media is the erosion of trust. Users are often sceptical about how their data is used, who has access to it and whether platforms are doing enough to protect them from cyber threats. The proposed framework rebuilds this trust by introducing mechanisms that assess user behaviour, identify potential threats and enforce strict privacy rules. When users feel that their interactions are monitored for safety without infringing on their privacy, they are more likely to participate openly and responsibly in online communities.

Malicious users such as spammers, imposters and misinformation agents pose serious risks to public safety, mental health and democratic processes. This research addresses these threats through multi-layered detection methods that accurately identify and isolate harmful actors while minimizing false accusations. By filtering out dangerous content and users, the system contributes to a healthier and more respectful digital environment, reducing the impact of online harassment, identity theft and propaganda.

In light of increasing public concern about data breaches and unethical data practices, this research aligns with global efforts to enforce data protection laws and ethical standards. It supports the principles outlined in regulations such as the General Data Protection Regulation (GDPR) by offering transparency, user consent and data minimization [20]. The framework demonstrates how technical solutions can uphold social values, ensuring that innovation does not come at the cost of personal rights.

As digital participation becomes a necessity for education, employment and civic engagement, ensuring a safe online space is more important than ever. This research provides a foundation for safer digital inclusion, particularly in regions or communities with limited digital literacy or exposure to cybersecurity measures. It helps bridge the trust gap between users and technology by placing privacy and security at the core of digital interactions. In conclusion, this research holds substantial social importance by fostering digital environments where individuals can interact, express and share with confidence and security. It not only advances technical safeguards but also reinforces the ethical and social responsibilities of digital platforms in protecting their users.

1.10. Organization of the Thesis

This thesis is structured into seven comprehensive chapters, each addressing a specific aspect of the research on privacy preservation in Online Social Media (OSM). The chapters are arranged to reflect a logical progression from understanding the problem context, through development of the proposed framework, to analysis of experimental results and final conclusions. The following is a brief overview of each chapter:

Chapter 1: Introduction

The first chapter introduces the research topic, outlining the growing relevance of privacy and security concerns in online social platforms. It presents the research problem, objectives, scope and significance of the study. The chapter also highlights the motivations behind the development of a multi-phase framework and summarizes the key contributions of the research. It establishes the foundation for the subsequent chapters by defining the context and the specific challenges addressed.

Chapter 2: Review of Literature

This chapter provides a detailed review of existing work related to privacy preservation, data protection and threat detection in social media environments. It examines various techniques such as anonymization, encryption, access control, trust evaluation and data mining. The review identifies strengths and limitations in current approaches and establishes the research gaps that the proposed framework aims to address. Comparative analysis of recent studies helps justify the need for a unified and layered solution.

Chapter 3: Development of a Trust-Based Behaviour Analysis Model (Phase I – TRIDENT)

Chapter 3 presents the design and implementation of the first phase of the framework, titled TRIDENT. This component focuses on assessing user trustworthiness by analysing behavioural patterns and interaction integrity. It describes how trust scores are computed using profile attributes, interaction histories and content verification. The chapter also explains the use of data mining techniques such as frequent pattern analysis, hybrid clustering and multi-layer classification to detect suspicious or malicious behaviour. The output of this phase is a classified set of users based on trust levels.

Chapter 4: Enforcement of Privacy-Centric Access Control through Attribute-Based Policies (Phase II – PRIVAFLOW)

This chapter introduces the second phase of the research, PRIVAFLOW, which enforces privacy rules for data contribution and access using enhanced attribute-based encryption and flow-graph validation. It details how data owners define privacy levels, how users are authenticated based on credentials and how access is granted only through valid trust relationships. The design of the Flow-Integrated Secure Attribute Retrieval Algorithm (FISARA) is explained, along with the techniques used to evaluate compatibility and enforce multi-level privacy controls.

Chapter 5: Deep Ensemble Detection Framework for Accurate Threat Classification (Phase III – DEEP-SECURE)

Chapter 5 focuses on the third and final phase, DEEP-SECURE. This component enhances detection accuracy using a layered ensemble model combining clustering, decision tree classification and kernel-based neural analysis. The chapter explains how each layer contributes to filtering user behaviour, reducing false positives and improving the reliability of threat identification. The Kernel-Enhanced Neural System for User Risk Evaluation (KENSURE) algorithm is described in detail, along with the integration of its modules for final user classification.

Chapter 6: Results and Discussion

This chapter presents the experimental results obtained from each phase of the framework. It includes quantitative evaluations of trust scores, privacy enforcement efficiency and threat classification accuracy. Comparative analysis with existing models is conducted across key performance metrics such as precision, recall, F1-score, processing time and detection rates. The results validate the effectiveness of the proposed framework and demonstrate its superiority in privacy preservation and threat mitigation. The discussion explores implications, limitations and insights drawn from the findings.

Chapter 7: Conclusion

The final chapter summarizes the research contributions and highlights how the proposed multi-phase framework addresses the core challenges of privacy and security in online social media. It revisits the objectives and outlines how each has been achieved. The chapter concludes with potential areas for future research, including the integration of additional privacy metrics, real-time deployment strategies and extensions to other digital ecosystems.

This structured organization ensures that each aspect of the research is thoroughly examined and logically presented, allowing readers to clearly understand the progression and impact of the proposed work.

1.11. Conclusion

This chapter provided an overview of the increasing significance of privacy preservation within Online Social Media (OSM) platforms. As these platforms continue to shape the way individuals communicate, share and consume information, they also introduce complex challenges related to data security and user privacy. The openness and interconnectedness of social networks make personal information vulnerable to various forms of misuse, including unauthorized access, identity theft, targeted manipulation and behavioural profiling. The chapter began by discussing the widespread use of social media and the types of data commonly shared by users. It emphasized the risks associated with the exposure of sensitive information, especially when privacy controls are inadequate or not well understood. The limitations of existing privacy mechanisms—such as basic visibility settings and static security models were outlined, highlighting the need for more robust, dynamic and user-focused solutions.

Furthermore, the chapter explored the challenges posed by the dynamic and relational structure of social networks, where data from one user can impact the privacy of another. These complexities demand advanced privacy-preserving approaches that take into account not only individual behaviour but also social context and data sensitivity. The motivation for the research was also presented, grounded in the need to develop a structured, reliable and adaptive framework that ensures secure data sharing, user protection and threat identification within OSM environments. The research aims to bridge the gap between privacy enforcement and usability, offering practical solutions that align with the evolving nature of online interaction. Finally, this chapter laid the foundation for the thesis by outlining the problem statement, research objectives and the broader significance of the work. It prepares the reader for the detailed examination of existing literature, system development and evaluation that follows in the subsequent chapters.

CHAPTER-II

LITERATURE REVIEW

2.1. Introduction

In the modern era of digital transformation, the proliferation of interconnected systems, social platforms, and smart devices has significantly altered how information is generated, shared, and managed. The exponential growth of digital footprints has led to an unprecedented accumulation of data, enabling the development of complex systems for surveillance, recommendation, personalization, and decision support. While these advancements promise efficiency and innovation across sectors, they simultaneously introduce critical challenges related to privacy, security, trust, and ethical governance. As societies become increasingly dependent on digital infrastructure, understanding and addressing these challenges has become a focal point for researchers and practitioners alike.

This literature review chapter aims to systematically examine scholarly efforts that have contributed to advancing knowledge across several interrelated domains, including data mining applications, privacy preservation techniques, cybersecurity strategies, digital forensics, educational monitoring frameworks, social media analysis, and decentralized system modelling. The objective is to synthesize key findings, identify methodological trends, and uncover existing limitations that hinder the development of responsible and robust technological systems.

The studies reviewed span a variety of disciplines, yet they are unified by common themes: the quest for meaningful insight from data, the need for secure and transparent systems, and the challenge of ensuring that emerging technologies align with societal values [21].A substantial body of work has emerged focusing on anomaly detection, fraud identification, behavioural prediction, and policy compliance across digital platforms. These studies often leverage statistical and computational models to detect irregularities, understand user behaviour, and recommend preventive measures. However, the practical implementation of these models in dynamic and diverse environments remains limited.

Another prominent theme in the literature is the evolving concept of privacy. In an age where user-generated content and digital interactions are pervasive, safeguarding personal information has become a pressing concern. Numerous approaches, including anonymization, differential privacy, edge perturbation, and access control mechanisms, have been proposed to protect user data while maintaining service utility. Despite these efforts, trade-offs between usability and confidentiality persist. Researchers continue to grapple with questions around data ownership, consent management, and context-aware policy enforcement, particularly in real-time and decentralized settings.

Cybersecurity, as another central pillar, has received considerable scholarly attention. With the increasing sophistication of cyber threats, there has been a shift toward developing proactive and adaptive defence mechanisms [22]. Studies reviewed in this chapter explore various intrusion detection systems, risk modelling techniques, and secure communication protocols designed to thwart unauthorized access and mitigate system vulnerabilities. Nevertheless, the effectiveness of these mechanisms often depends on timely updates, large-scale adoption, and compatibility with legacy systems—factors that are not always adequately addressed in current frameworks.

In addition to these technical dimensions, the review considers literature on the socio-technical aspects of system design and adoption. As digital tools permeate sectors such as education, healthcare, and governance, there is growing concern about ethical surveillance, digital equity, and psychological impacts of technology use. Studies focusing on educational environments highlight the potential of learning analytics and performance monitoring tools, yet they also point to concerns over student privacy, algorithmic bias, and over-surveillance. Similarly, the use of data-driven methods to infer mental health conditions from social media activity raises questions about user consent, stigmatization, and data misuse.

Decentralized systems, such as those based on blockchain technology and federated learning principles, are increasingly presented as alternatives to centralized control structures. These systems promise enhanced user autonomy, thrustless transactions, and resilience against single points of failure [23]. However, research also indicates unresolved challenges related to scalability, governance, interoperability, and user comprehension. Ensuring that such systems are not only technically sound but also socially acceptable remains an open issue.

To facilitate a coherent understanding of the landscape, this chapter organizes the literature into thematic categories based on the primary objectives of the studies, such as privacy protection, behaviour modelling, data analysis, cybersecurity, and system resilience. Each section critically evaluates the contributions of selected studies, drawing attention to their methodological strengths, application contexts, and practical limitations.

The chapter concludes by synthesizing key insights and identifying gaps that necessitate further investigation. These gaps highlight the need for holistic frameworks that balance technological advancement with ethical imperatives, user empowerment, and long-term sustainability. By mapping the existing body of knowledge and highlighting areas requiring deeper exploration, this literature review lays the groundwork for the development of a research framework that is not only innovative but also aligned with the needs of diverse stakeholders in an increasingly complex digital environment.

2.2. Review on Data Mining for social media and its Techniques

The increasing volume and complexity of data generated across digital and physical environments have necessitated the development of novel data-driven methodologies for extracting meaningful insights. From multidimensional time series to textual and behavioral data sourced through online platforms, researchers are leveraging innovative techniques to enhance interpretability, efficiency, and application scope across disciplines. The reviewed studies encompass a diverse range of topics, including time series transformation, waste reduction through second-hand commerce, anomaly detection in social networks, educational performance analysis, word sense disambiguation, consumer behaviour in the organic food market, and global social media trends. Each study contributes to addressing real-world challenges by adopting structured analytical approaches that improve decision-making, optimize resource use, and deepen understanding of human and system behavior. Together, they underscore the growing significance of integrative and adaptive methods in the evolving landscape of data mining and its practical implications.

Tiwari, D., & Kumar, M. (2019) [24] present a structured survey that maps common data-mining tasks (classification, clustering, sentiment analysis, topic modeling, link analysis) to their applicability in online social networks. The paper is useful as a primer: it highlights pre-processing challenges (noise, slang, code-mixing), standard feature representations (bag-of-words, embeddings), and evaluation metrics commonly used for social content. A strength is its clear taxonomy that helps new researchers choose methods based on data type and goal. Limitations include relatively shallow treatment of recent deep representation methods and limited discussion of privacy-preserving considerations; future work should link technique selection to ethical and scalability constraints.

Ali, F., El-Sappagh, S., Islam, S. R., et al. (2021)[25] proposes a cloud-based big-data analytics framework that fuses physiological time series from wearables with user-generated health content on social platforms to improve abnormality detection. Methodologically it combines ontology-driven semantic enrichment, dimensionality reduction, and bidirectional long short-term memory models for temporal classification. Reported results indicate improved classification of conditions such as diabetes and hypertension when heterogeneous sources are integrated. The work is strong on system design and multimodal fusion but would benefit from clearer discussion of dataset scale, real-world deployment constraints (latency, privacy consent), and external validation beyond the reported experiments.

Li, X., Xie, Q., Jiang, J., Zhou, Y., & Huang, L. (2019) [26] and colleagues propose a hybrid methodology that combines patent landscape analysis with microblogging signals to trace the emergence and public perception of a technology (perovskite solar cells). The study shows complementary strengths: patents reveal technological maturation and inventor networks, while social data capture stakeholder attention, sentiment, and topical shifts. Their comparison uncovers temporal offsets between technical milestones and public discussion, demonstrating how social signals can augment foresight. Limitations include platform bias (Twitter user demographics) and the case-study focus; broader multi-platform validation would strengthen generalizability.

Wang et al., (2020) [27] deliver a comprehensive review of deep models applied to spatio-temporal tasks, categorizing data types (trajectories, event sequences, grid-structured signals) and mapping architectures (RNNs, CNNs, graph neural networks, attention mechanisms) to tasks such as prediction, anomaly detection, and classification. The survey synthesizes application domains—transportation, urban planning, health monitoring—and outlines key modeling challenges: multi-scale dependencies, irregular sampling, and interpretability. The paper's thorough taxonomy and discussion of future directions (modeling of heterogeneity, robustness) make it a valuable reference, though empirical guidance on model selection for resource-constrained settings is limited.

Liao et al. (2024)[28] investigate user profiles and behavioural patterns on TikTok, focusing on how user-generated content (UGC) influences social media application development. The study targets Taiwanese users and applies clustering and association rule mining on survey data (N = 2,011) stored in a relational database. Results yield distinct behavioural clusters and rule-based patterns, highlighting how interactive elements of UGC support social app evolution and engagement. The findings underscore TikTok's potential in shaping social media trends and stress the need for extended research in other contexts.

Zheng et al. (2024)[29] conduct a thorough analysis of international tax risk detection methods, identifying 14 unique approaches categorized into relationship-based and non-relationship-based techniques. These methods aim to counteract the fiscal and systemic impacts of tax evasion. The study further explores technical limitations such as fragmented fiscal knowledge, poor interpretability of results, and heavy dependence on annotated datasets. The authors propose that integrating data-driven systems with structured fiscal knowledge can advance the evolution of tax monitoring frameworks.

Rawat et al. (2024) [30]review methodologies for detecting hate speech in social media, categorizing 66 studies between 2018 and 2023. The research outlines five primary classification approaches: traditional machine learning, deep networks, ensemble models, graph-based methods, and hybrid graph systems. It also emphasizes the practical relevance of labeled datasets and points out persisting limitations, such as contextual ambiguities and evolving language patterns. The paper calls for expanded investigations to overcome the unresolved hurdles in moderating harmful content.

Lian et al. (2024)[31] analyze public sentiment in China concerning a newly popular language-based tool through 96,435 comments and 55,186 reposts from social media platforms. The study employs text mining to reveal themes focused on productivity, workplace changes, and educational applications, along with concerns about misinformation, job displacement, and human–technology interaction. The analysis indicates that public opinion is largely shaped by decentralized discourse rather than traditional media, informing policy and communication strategies.

Naval et al. (2024) [32]explore how data mining can enhance targeted advertising by analysing patterns in user profiles and activity logs. They discuss methodologies like clustering, classification, and association rules to tailor promotional content based on individual preferences. The study also touches on how adaptive advertising systems respond to real-time feedback, increasing the relevance and engagement of advertisements. Examples of current systems are presented to support the practicality of the proposed techniques.

Alsemaree et al. (2024)[33] address the complexity of analysing Arabic-language sentiment due to its intricate grammatical structure. Focusing on reviews of coffee products from Twitter (N = 10,646), the study applies TF-IDF and MRMR techniques for feature extraction, followed by classification using support vector machines, decision trees, random forests, and k-nearest neighbor. Ensemble learning further improves accuracy, achieving over 95% in prediction performance. These results demonstrate the method's applicability in assessing consumer perception within niche markets.

Nemati et al. (2024)[34] propose an anomaly detection model combining support vector machines with feature selection via genetic algorithms and gray wolf optimization. Their approach processes financial data streams from selected companies (2014–2020), identifying crucial financial ratios linked to abnormal behaviour. The optimized model improves detection metrics, achieving an accuracy of 75.83% and precision of 66.80%. The study underscores the potential of integrating data stream processing with optimization techniques for financial and cybersecurity applications.

Shahriar and Dara (2024)[35] introduce a structured framework and pipeline designed to mitigate privacy risks in analysing social media texts. The framework identifies six categories of privacy threats and integrates protection protocols throughout data collection and processing stages. A case study using Facebook data shows that their method reduces author identification accuracy by 13.64% while retaining functional performance for topic modeling and sentiment analysis. This work offers a systematic approach to safeguarding personal information in social text analytics.

Abuashour and MKA (2024) [36]assess the effectiveness of three data mining platformsWEKA, Orange, and RapidMiner—on classification tasks across three datasets: Iris, Car Evaluation, and Tic-Tac-Toe Endgame. Four classification algorithmsDecision Tree, Naïve Bayes, Neural Network, and Random Forestare employed to analyze variations in accuracy. Findings highlight that model performance is influenced by the interplay of dataset size, algorithm choice, and software platform, offering guidance for selecting suitable tools for specific predictive analytics tasks.

Yan et al. (2024)[37] present a model for extracting meaningful patterns from multidimensional time series by transforming them into linear sequences of spatial events. This method emphasizes the complex interrelations among variables through a variable-length tuple mining technique. Unlike conventional models, the approach does not require extensive labeled data, making it widely applicable. The model's effectiveness is demonstrated in motion classification tasks, where it outperforms traditional methods in recognizing intricate patterns. Potential uses include system monitoring in IT environments, tracking physiological signals in healthcare, and interpreting user interactions in online platforms.

Badran et al. (2025)[38] explore the reuse of consumer goods as a central strategy in promoting circular economy principles. Through the analysis of over 1,000 images from Instagram thrift shops in Lebanon, the study identifies the most commonly reused items—primarily textiles, apparel, and footwear. By comparing environmental outcomes using life cycle assessments, the study finds that reused items generally replace new products and thus reduce production-related resource consumption. Although reuse outperforms recycling, items such as electronics and furniture show lower reuse frequencies. The study also discusses the practical benefits of digital tools in promoting efficient waste management and sustainable consumption behaviours.

Zhang (2025)[39] introduces a technique for identifying abnormal profiles in social networks by combining graph-based encoders and attention mechanisms. The model dynamically aggregates features from neighboring nodes and detects anomalies by measuring reconstruction deviations. It is tested on a real-world Facebook network dataset and shows better classification results compared to other network models. Performance is evaluated using various metrics including AUC and F1-score. The method is efficient on large datasets and holds promise for applications in security monitoring and financial oversight. Future development may include privacy-preserving and distributed learning techniques to expand its usability.

Praveen Kumar et al. (2025)[40] propose a computational model aimed at predicting student academic performance by processing educational records through a deep learning structure. The approach includes pre-processing, feature extraction, classification, and evaluation. Feature representation is enhanced using textual analysis techniques such as Word 2Vec and Inverse Gravity Moment. The classification model incorporates a gated bidirectional memory-based network with convolutional layers to analyze behavioural patterns, especially the influence of social media usage. Empirical results indicate strong performance in prediction accuracy, with the analysis showing that excessive weekday use of social platforms correlates with reduced academic achievement.

Hung et al. (2025)[41] introduce a method to address the problem of ambiguous word meanings by modeling lexical relationships as social networks. Words are treated as nodes, and their co-occurrences form interaction links. By identifying words with high connectivity across distinct communities, the model infers multiple meanings and assigns context-specific interpretations. The approach is tested on a movie review dataset and demonstrates improved understanding of polysemous words without relying on manually labeled data. This unsupervised structure improves the precision of textual analysis, making it effective in fields where language ambiguity poses a challenge.

Vo et al. (2025)[42] examine consumer preferences for organic food by extracting key themes from social media posts and applying conjoint analysis to quantify decision-making criteria. Using Vietnamese consumer responses, the study finds that sustainability is the most valued attribute, followed by organic certification, pricing, shelf-life, and country of origin. The analysis highlights two distinct consumer groups: one prioritizes environmental sustainability while the other focuses on organic production practices. By leveraging online discourse, the research demonstrates how digital platforms can be used to identify evolving consumer expectations and guide market strategies in the organic food sector.

Khan et al. (2025)[43] examine the rapid global spread of internet access and mobile device usage, particularly smartphones, as a driver for the growing role of social media in daily life. Their analysis underscores how real-time platforms have created opportunities for billions of people to interact, share, and engage across borders. The study highlights global adoption trends—especially in developing countries—and notes how these technologies have become essential in areas like urban planning, communication, and commerce. The widespread use of social platforms now presents both opportunities and challenges for data-driven insights into public behaviour.

Collectively, these studies demonstrate the versatility and impact of advanced data analysis techniques across multiple sectors. Whether improving pattern recognition in complex datasets, promoting sustainable consumption, identifying irregularities in network behaviour, or understanding consumer preferences and language use, each work offers a targeted solution to a specific challenge. The integration of innovative modeling approaches with domain-specific knowledge not only enhances analytical accuracy but also fosters broader societal benefits, from environmental conservation to educational development and public safety. These contributions reaffirm the importance of continuous methodological refinement and interdisciplinary collaboration in harnessing data for informed decision-making and meaningful progress across fields.

2.3. Review on Privacy Protection Online Social Media Network

In the digital era, social networking platforms have become embedded in everyday life, transforming communication, interaction, and information exchange across social, political, and economic domains. As users increasingly share personal, visual, and behavioural data online, concerns regarding privacy protection and data security have escalated. This has prompted extensive academic inquiry into understanding how privacy information is propagated, managed, and perceived in online social environments. The studies reviewed here reflect a growing body of literature that investigates the dynamics of privacy disclosure, user behaviour, regulatory gaps, and technical solutions in social networking contexts. Drawing on recent findings from a diverse set of disciplines, this synthesis aims to explore the complexities of digital privacy and offer insights into safeguarding personal information in interconnected digital spaces.

Siddula, M., Li, L., & Li, Y. (2018) [44]empirically examine the effectiveness of common anonymization and perturbation strategies on network data and user attributes. The study quantifies re-identification risk under various adversary models and shows that straightforward de-identification often leaves residual linkability through structural cues. The work's empirical orientation is valuable for practitioners designing release mechanisms; however, its experiments use a limited set of datasets and adversary assumptions, so extensions to dynamic networks and cross-platform linkages are necessary to reflect modern threat models.

Wang, X., Ning, Z., Zhou, M., et al. (2018)[45] examines privacy challenges unique to vehicular social networks (VSNs), where mobility, ephemeral connectivity, and safety requirements complicate content sharing. The authors classify threats (identity/linkage attacks, location inference) and review cryptographic, pseudonym-based, and policy-driven solutions, emphasizing trade-offs between privacy, latency, and routing efficiency. The article is comprehensive for the VSN domain, but many proposed schemes remain untested in large-scale deployments; future work must reconcile real-time safety needs with rigorous privacy guarantees.

Hu, X., Zhu, T., Zhai, X., Zhou, W., & Zhao, W. (2021)[46] investigates how private information diffuses across a social platform and demonstrates measurable differences between diffusion patterns of private versus public content. Using graph convolutional models to trace propagation, the authors identify structural and temporal markers that predict privacy leakage. They then propose mitigation strategies aimed at reducing unintended spread. The study's strength is grounding in real-world traces and use of modern graph methods; open questions remain around user perception of interventions and how mitigation impacts legitimate information flows.

Srivatsan, S., & Maheswari, N. (2022) [47] propose an optimization framework that applies evolutionary algorithms to search for anonymization transformations satisfying k-anonymity, l-diversity, and t-closeness while minimizing information loss. The approach explicitly balances privacy constraints against utility for downstream analytics. The paper contributes a novel optimization angle and empirical comparisons showing favorable trade-offs. A limitation is computational cost for large graphs and potential sensitivity to parameter tuning; scalability and robustness evaluations on larger, more heterogeneous networks would strengthen practical applicability.

Luo et al. (2025)[48] investigate the propagation of privacy-related information on Weibo, a leading microblogging platform in China. The authors introduce a privacy propagation reconstruction method (W-PIPPR) and generate a dataset (PIPD-Weibo) to analyze the diffusion dynamics. Their findings suggest that both the sensitivity of the disclosed content and the influence of the individual sharing it significantly affect the reach and speed of dissemination. The study highlights the importance of identifying key factors and topological patterns in privacy propagation to inform policy and technological frameworks for social media governance.

Darwish (2025)[49] provides a foundational overview of security and privacy essentials in the context of social networking platforms. The chapter outlines the evolution of user engagement across domains such as education, entertainment, and business, while emphasizing the inherent risks of data exposure. The work stresses the importance of protecting users' personal data through robust security protocols and policy enforcement to ensure safe and responsible digital interaction.

Ahmed and Lee (2025)[50] examine the dual impact of social media use and privacy concerns on political engagement. Through empirical studies conducted in Singapore and the United States, the authors find that while frequent exposure to political content increases participation, heightened privacy concerns can negate this effect. The study underscores the psychological conflict between digital expression and data vulnerability, with lower cognitive ability further amplifying privacy-related withdrawal from online discourse.

Zhao et al. (2025)[51] provide a comprehensive review of visual content privacy, proposing a three-pronged framework that addresses privacy threats from computer vision, human vision, or both. The survey categorizes techniques designed to obscure sensitive visual data, evaluates their effectiveness, and identifies unresolved challenges. The authors call for broader, unified strategies that transcend isolated use cases to better secure visual content shared in digital environments.

Srihita et al. (2025)[52] explore the role of computational tools in enhancing content customization and moderation on social platforms. The chapter discusses how personalization mechanisms support user experience while also raising ethical concerns, particularly regarding the misuse of automated systems to manipulate or extract user data. The authors emphasize the need for transparent guidelines and accountable usage of technology to prevent violations of individual privacy.

Teepapal (2025)[53] evaluates how personalized digital marketing influences user engagement through a structured stimulus-organism-response (S-O-

R) model. The research shows that while customized interactions build trust and perceived usefulness, they also prompt concern over personal data exposure. Notably, these concerns do not directly hinder user engagement, suggesting that utility and trust can mitigate privacy apprehensions. The study highlights the importance of balancing personalization with ethical data practices in online commerce.

Thomas (2025)[54] discusses the use of social media in online education, emphasizing its capacity to foster collaboration, trust, and community among learners. Drawing from theories of social presence and community of inquiry, the chapter examines strategies to promote transparency and inclusivity while addressing privacy-related risks. It offers best practices for leveraging digital platforms to support educational engagement without compromising learner confidentiality.

Heinrich and Gerhart (2025)[55] delve into the gap between stated privacy concerns and actual user behaviour. Their study builds on privacy boundary theory and analyzes responses from a survey that assessed perceived sensitivity and user knowledge. The findings identify five distinct user profiles based on privacy attitudes, revealing widespread confusion about effective protective measures. The authors argue for greater digital literacy initiatives to align privacy awareness with protective actions.

Zhao et al. (2025)[56] propose a reversible image degradation approach for managing privacy in smart city environments. This method allows for privacy-preserving visual data collection while retaining usability through adjustable resolution. The approach incorporates cryptographic techniques to enhance security and demonstrates effectiveness in balancing privacy and operational needs within urban monitoring systems. The study contributes to the growing need for privacy-aware technologies in smart infrastructure.

Gong et al. (2025)[57] propose a privacy-focused collaborative learning framework that allows for the integration of diverse data sources without the need for central data aggregation. This method is particularly suited to environments where data remains distributed across multiple devices or institutions. To address inconsistencies among datasets, the authors introduce an adaptive integration approach that aligns disparate features into a common representation space through a statistical alignment process and multi-view learning. The framework further incorporates robust privacy safeguards by using encryption and anonymization measures at various stages: data preprocessing, model training, and output generation. These include techniques such as secure computation, homomorphic encryption, and feature de-identification. Evaluation using real-world datasets demonstrates improved predictive accuracy and resilience compared to traditional decentralized learning approaches, emphasizing the system's practical utility and enhanced privacy safeguards.

Whelan et al. (2025)[58] re-examine the widely discussed privacy paradox, in which users knowingly disclose personal data online despite acknowledging privacy concerns. The authors challenge the prevailing notion that such behaviour stems primarily from user apathy or convenience. Using survey and interview data from Facebook users, they test the influence of psychological traits—particularly external locus of control—on disclosure behaviour. While quantitative analysis suggests that laziness does not significantly alter the relationship between concern and behaviour, qualitative findings reveal some user tendencies that align with convenience-driven sharing. The study ultimately concludes that individuals who perceive external factors as more influential in controlling their digital environment are more likely to exhibit contradictory behaviour regarding privacy, highlighting the need to expand the explanatory framework beyond simplistic behavioural assumptions.

Ekinci et al. (2025)[59] explore the negative consequences of influencer culture in online platforms, particularly focusing on how unethical conduct by social media figures can mislead audiences and distort commercial practices. The research identifies six core themes: promotion of harmful goods, spread of misinformation, pressure from unattainable beauty standards, emotional strain due to comparisons, manipulation through deceptive marketing, and issues of personal data misuse. The study underscores the psychological and behavioural toll such influencers can exert on audiences and calls attention to regulatory blind spots. The authors present a set of guiding propositions and research questions aimed at examining these harms from multidisciplinary perspectives, stressing the importance of ethical oversight in influencer-driven marketing strategies.

Xing et al. (2025)[60] investigate public attitudes toward remote work during the COVID-19 pandemic by analysing conversations on Twitter. Applying principles from justice theory, the authors distinguish between two perspectives in the discourse: personal benefits versus organizational and societal impacts. The analysis reveals a pattern in which users expressing strong emotional responseseither favourable or unfavourabletend to frame their opinions around perceived fairness or unfairness. The study uses clustering and sentiment tracking techniques to chart topic evolution and identify justice-oriented concerns such as equitable treatment and transparent communication. The results suggest that fairness perceptions significantly influence user sentiment on workplace transformation, with distributive and interpersonal fairness emerging as distinct yet interconnected themes.

Haque et al. (2025)[61] assess how users respond to personalized content recommendations on social media, focusing on the clarity and usefulness of these suggestions. The study examines user expectations regarding transparency and the need for meaningful explanations when encountering unfamiliar content. Feedback from Facebook users highlights a preference for concise and easily understandable justifications over technical or opaque descriptions. Participants indicated that clarity in recommendations improves their trust and comfort with the platform. The research offers a synthesized framework for designing user-centred explanation systems that emphasize control, relevance, and interpretability. It also outlines how these explanation elements influence perceptions of trustworthiness and ease of use in digital interactions.

Iam-On et al. (2025)[62] present a novel ensemble clustering strategy aimed at extracting patterns from user-generated social data while maintaining data confidentiality. Targeting applications such as tourism recommendation systems, their framework divides datasets into manageable segments and generates multiple clustering configurations to better represent each segment. This approach not only enhances the accuracy of the grouping but also reduces the computational burden. Unlike conventional single-pass methods, their multi-level design accommodates the volume and variability of online feedback while incorporating privacy-sensitive mechanisms. Experimental results on tourism-related datasets show that the proposed technique consistently performs better than comparable clustering methods and remains effective even under data noise and scale variations.

The reviewed studies collectively underscore the complexity and urgency of safeguarding privacy in social media contexts. From theoretical models and user perceptions to technical frameworks and ethical considerations, each contribution offers unique insights into how digital privacy can be better understood, protected, and regulated. As digital communication becomes increasingly visual, personalized, and ubiquitous, the tension between connectivity and confidentiality grows more pronounced. Effective solutions must therefore integrate user education, policy innovation, and technical robustness to navigate the evolving landscape of privacy in networked societies. Continued interdisciplinary research is essential for crafting holistic strategies that respect individual rights while supporting digital participation.

2.4. Review on Algorithms for Privacy Protection in Online Social Media Networks

As digital platforms become increasingly embedded in everyday life, the need to understand the evolving challenges related to privacy, security, and responsible data practices has grown significantly. This collection of academic reviews brings together recent scholarly efforts from diverse domains including social media governance, online consumer behavior, distributed systems, vehicular networks, and mobile sensing technologies to explore how personal data is collected, managed, and protected. The studies reviewed highlight critical concerns such as unauthorized surveillance, information leakage, regulatory impacts, ethical decision-making, and the social consequences of digital fatigue. By examining technical advancements, behavioral insights, and regulatory frameworks, these reviews offer a well-rounded understanding of how data-related risks are being addressed across sectors. Collectively, they reflect a growing urgency to establish safeguards that respect individual rights while enabling innovation and efficiency in connected environments.

Jain, A. K., Sahoo, S. R., &Kaubiyal, J. (2021) [63]survey threats and defenses across the OSN stack, covering content privacy, malicious accounts, inference attacks, and proposed countermeasures (access control models, anomaly detection, cryptographic techniques). The contribution lies in synthesizing diverse approaches and identifying persistent gaps—notably cross-platform inference and usability of privacy controls. The review calls for evaluative benchmarks and standardized datasets to compare defenses, a recommendation that remains relevant for aligning research with operational needs.

Zhang, Z., & Gupta, B. B. (2018) [64] analyze threats to data integrity and trust on social platforms, discussing misinformation, bot networks, and content tampering detection. The paper proposes a layered architecture combining provenance tracking, user reputation models, and automated content verification to improve trustworthiness. Its strength is in framing security and trust as intertwined problems requiring socio-technical solutions; empirical validation of the proposed evaluation metrics and integration strategies remains an avenue for future work.

Agrawal et al. (2024)[65] explore how decentralized technologies like blockchain can address various issues prevalent in online social platforms. These include concerns such as unauthorized data access, identity manipulation, and misinformation. The study outlines blockchain's potential in enhancing transparency, data integrity, and user control, while also highlighting practical barriers such as scalability and interoperability challenges that must be overcome for broader adoption.

Sun et al. (2024)[66] present a comprehensive overview of privacy and security vulnerabilities in Internet of Things (IoT) environments, particularly those intersecting with social systems. They assess common risks such as flawed firmware, insecure protocols, and inadequate access controls. The article proposes a multi-layered protection strategy, including blockchain-enhanced access models and legal frameworks, to strengthen user privacy in an interconnected world.

Manoharan (2024)[67] investigates strategies that streamline user interaction on social platforms through task automation. The study examines various digital tools designed to increase visibility and audience interaction through structured posting and engagement tactics. Results indicate that consistent and optimized automation techniques contribute significantly to increased user participation and brand loyalty.

Habib et al. (2024) [68]focus on the detection of deceptive user profiles within social networks. They analyze the behavioural and structural characteristics often associated with fake accounts, such as reused profile pictures and spam-like content. The research categorizes detection techniques based on their reliance on content analysis, user behaviour metrics, and profile metadata, providing a consolidated view of current detection methodologies.

Voorveld et al. (2024)[69] examine user responses to algorithm-driven advertising on social platforms. Based on a Dutch user survey, four distinct consumer groups were identified, each varying in awareness, skepticism, and coping strategies. The findings underline the necessity for tailored communication strategies and regulatory interventions to safeguard user autonomy in digital marketing contexts.

Kong and Ding (2024)[70] discuss the implications of social media background checks in recruitment. The authors review how publicly shared content influences employment decisions, often raising ethical and privacy concerns. The paper suggests establishing clearer guidelines for employers and educational programs for job seekers to manage their digital presence responsibly.

Jethava and Rao (2024)[71] provide a detailed review of security risks such as profile cloning and multi-account (Sybil) attacks in digital communities. The study emphasizes that beyond technical solutions, trust mechanisms among users are vital. A taxonomy of trust evaluation techniques is presented, along with recommendations for enhancing platform security through community-based trust-building models.

Zhang et al. (2024)[72] propose a robust model that enhances the resilience of collaborative data processing systems within social platforms. Their approach merges data integrity techniques with fault tolerance methods to mitigate disruptions from untrustworthy sources. By incorporating similarity-based filtering, their method efficiently eliminates inconsistencies, improving both reliability and performance.

Khan et al. (2024)[73] address the procedural gaps in digital forensics related to social platforms. They suggest a dual-chain model incorporating both local and global threat separation and refined data handling protocols. This structure enhances evidence traceability and supports systematic investigations across heterogeneous digital environments.

Li et al. (2025)[74] introduce a privacy-preserving system for image sharing within digital communities. They propose a dual-framework model that enables secure group communication by leveraging encryption strategies resistant to content compression. Their system also features fast processing speeds, making it viable for large-scale implementation across various platforms.

Huang (2025)[75] discusses the growing tension between technological advancement and privacy in digital society. The article attributes privacy erosion to legal loopholes, user negligence, and systemic vulnerabilities. Suggested remedies include stricter regulations, advanced protective technologies, and comprehensive public awareness initiatives to promote responsible internet usage and reinforce individual privacy rights.

Uwayezu et al. (2025)[76] examined the public's perception of privacy risks linked to social media platforms that offer complimentary services. The study focused on how users reconcile the advantages of personalized content and platform access with growing concerns about data monitoring. Utilizing insights from internet privacy specialists, the research found that while users benefit from cost-free platforms, increased understanding of how their activities are analyzed has intensified their concerns regarding data use. The findings underscore the need for platform operators and policymakers to strike a better balance between enhancing user experience and safeguarding personal data.

He et al. (2025)[77] conducted a comprehensive overview of rumor dynamics within social networks, addressing both psychological and structural mechanisms behind their spread. The article distinguishes between various rumor propagation models and evaluates strategies for identifying and mitigating false information, especially within immersive virtual environments. It also emphasizes the challenges posed by digital content manipulation and automated accounts. The authors advocate for combined efforts through public awareness, regulatory initiatives, and advanced tracking techniques to address these issues systematically.

Liu et al. (2025)[78] provided a systematic assessment of integrated data sources used in smart city initiatives, particularly within real estate management. The review covers technical methods for merging data from urban sensors, public feedback, and spatial datasets. It identifies persistent challenges such as inconsistent data quality and the protection of sensitive information. The authors recommend developing robust frameworks that enhance decision-making and resource allocation while ensuring that interdisciplinary collaboration and information privacy remain priorities.

Liu et al. (2025)[79] proposed a methodology that merges data protection protocols with statistical modeling to improve confidentiality during data processing. The approach ensures equitable data representation and leverages privacy-preserving mechanisms to secure the analysis outcomes. The model was tested on publicly available datasets, demonstrating its reliability in balancing prediction accuracy with data confidentiality. The results suggest that the proposed solution is well-suited for contexts requiring high levels of privacy without compromising analytical performance.

Weng (2025)[80] addressed the challenges associated with limited storage and data privacy in distributed network environments. The research introduced an optimized caching strategy based on collaborative learning principles, combining centralized oversight with local execution. Results showed that this approach significantly improved caching efficiency and reduced system strain while maintaining user confidentiality. The methodology also demonstrated superior speed and scalability compared to conventional data-sharing models, particularly in high-traffic conditions.

Zhao (2025)[81] designed a monitoring system for domestic environments that minimizes visual data exposure during video analysis. The system integrates selective data capture with behaviour recognition to ensure user discretion. Experimental evaluations across several multimedia databases confirmed the system's ability to retain high accuracy in behaviour interpretation while protecting visual privacy. This research highlights practical applications for domestic security and monitoring technologies where discretion and efficiency are critical.

Wang et al. (2025)[82] developed a framework for safeguarding information collected through mobile crowd sensing platforms, especially when handling diverse data formats. Their approach uses cross-referencing and secure computation techniques to ensure data integrity during storage and transmission. A verification mechanism was incorporated to confirm the completeness and authenticity of submitted data without revealing its content. The method proved effective in securing heterogeneous data while maintaining low processing costs.

Yang and Liu (2025)[83] investigated the regulatory effects of data protection laws on market structures in the online platform ecosystem. Through comparative analysis using longitudinal data, the study found that regulatory measures led to a temporary reduction in market dominance by leading firms. However, the influence of such policies weakened over time, indicating the adaptive nature of digital platforms to policy shifts. The paper contributes valuable insights into how policy instruments can temporarily reshape competition in digital markets.

Shang and Deng (2025)[84] proposed a decentralized method for managing data exchanges in vehicular communication networks. Their framework uses a layered validation process that assigns roles to network participants based on trustworthiness. Records of interactions are maintained through a tamper-resistant system, enabling reliable auditing and traceability. Performance tests confirmed the method's resilience against various network threats and its ability to improve the reliability and security of automotive data exchanges.

Wang et al. (2025)[85] explored the psychological and behavioural roots of data protection fatigue, a state where users disengage from privacy practices due to overload or resignation. Applying a framework that maps stress-related responses to behavioural outcomes, the study revealed three distinct patterns leading to such fatigue. These patterns include rational evaluations, emotional strain, and overload-induced withdrawal. The findings offer a nuanced perspective on how privacy apathy develops and provide guidance for improving engagement in privacy practices.

Kim and Zo (2025)[86] examined how awareness of constant tracking affects individuals' willingness to share personal preferences in digital content platforms. Their analysis revealed that people who perceive themselves as being observed are more likely to question the value of revealing personal data. Paradoxically, those who recognize the value of their data may either overshare or become overly cautious. The study outlines this tension as a key design challenge for content delivery systems, which must accommodate user privacy without degrading personalization.

The insights drawn from these studies underscore the complexity of ensuring data security and privacy in the digital era. Whether addressing algorithmic transparency, behavioural tracking, content moderation, or decentralized data exchange, each study contributes valuable perspectives on how to manage personal information responsibly. Key themes such as user awareness, trust-building, regulation, and ethical system design recur throughout the reviews, pointing to the need for integrated solutions that balance utility with protection. As digital interactions become more immersive and data-intensive, continued research and dialogue are essential to adapt protective strategies that are both effective and equitable. These reviews not only map current progress but also call attention to ongoing gaps and future directions in safeguarding data integrity and user autonomy in a rapidly transforming digital landscape.

2.5. Review on Frameworks for Security in social media using Data Mining Techniques

Social media influencers play an instrumental role in promoting awareness for public interest causes. **Mouhssine, E., & Khalid, C. (2018)** [87] propose a pipeline that ingests public textual posts, applies filtering and sentiment analysis, then classifies content for extremism using supervised learning. The framework emphasizes streaming collection via platform APIs and an architecture intended to support analysts with flagged content. The paper is pragmatic and addresses a critical use case, but it lacks detailed treatment of false positive rates, bias in training data, and safeguards against misuse of surveillance capabilities; transparency and ethical controls should be integral to deployment.

Sandhu, A. K. (2021) [88] surveys cloud-based big data ecosystems and maps common processing frameworks (MapReduce, Spark) to storage and service models. The discussion highlights security and governance issues—data residency, access control, and encryption in transit/at rest—while calling attention to heterogeneity of data sources typical in social media analytics. The review is a practical resource for architects, though it remains high-level; concrete design patterns for secure, privacy-aware analytic pipelines would add implementation value.

Souri, A., & Hosseini, R. (2018)[89] categorize malware detection approaches into signature-based and behavior-based classes, survey feature extraction methods, and compare classifiers used in practice. Their analysis underscores the advantage of behavior-driven models for zero-day detection and highlights challenges when adversaries employ evasion tactics. For social platforms, mapping these insights to content and account behavior (rather than binary executables) suggests promising directions but requires adaptation of feature design and evaluation to social data peculiarities.

Cordeiro, Lopezosa, and Guallar (2025)[90] introduce the Data Analysis Framework for Information and Media (DAFIM), a comprehensive methodology for analysing textual data from digital media platforms. The framework encompasses data collection via APIs and web scraping, preprocessing, and enrichment techniques such as named entity recognition and sentiment analysis. A case study focusing on the Israel–Lebanon conflict demonstrates DAFIM's capability to uncover narrative patterns and detect clickbait, highlighting its applicability in various digital contexts.

Elly et al. (2025) [91]address the escalating issue of fraud in e-commerce by developing a framework that leverages machine learning and data mining techniques for real-time detection. The proposed system is designed to handle large data volumes, identify anomalies, and provide timely alerts, thereby enhancing the security and trustworthiness of online transactions.

Yuan and Xue (2025)[92] propose an integrated framework that combines various media typestext, images, and videosfor comprehensive information extraction and value mining. By employing advanced techniques such as convolutional neural networks and graph neural networks, the framework enhances the processing and analysis of complex multimedia data, with potential applications in fields like healthcare and security.

Razaque et al. (2025)[93] conduct an extensive review of malicious code detection within data mining applications, analysing 167 publications from 2008 to 2024. The study identifies vulnerabilities in machine learning algorithms and emphasizes the need for robust detection methods to mitigate risks associated with malicious code, particularly in sectors like telecommunications and bioinformatics.

Mbimbi, Murray, and Wilson (2025)[94] present a secure digital evidence management framework that combines zero-knowledge proofs with private blockchain technology. This approach ensures whistleblower anonymity while maintaining the integrity and authenticity of submitted evidence, offering a significant advancement in the protection of informants in sensitive disclosures.

Ahsun, Khan Sio, and Winner (2025)[95] develop a data management framework tailored for enhanced financial forecasting using big data analytics. The framework integrates advanced data processing techniques, scalable storage solutions, and high-performance computing to improve trend prediction, risk assessment, and decision-making in financial markets.

Wang (2024)[96] explores topic mining and information security analysis on social media platforms using big data and deep convolutional neural networks. The study demonstrates improved accuracy in identifying security-related topics and potential threats, contributing to the development of more secure social networking environments.

Surabhi et al. (2024)[97] introduce a hybrid detection framework that combines deep learning and data mining techniques to identify manipulated images in digital media. The approach enhances the accuracy of detecting faux content, addressing the growing concern of misinformation and digital security.

Javed et al. (2024) [98]design and implement an enterprise office automation system based on a web service framework and data mining techniques. The system aims to improve operational efficiency by automating administrative tasks and integrating various business processes, thereby enhancing decision-making and productivity.

Abdillah et al. (2024)[99] examine the interplay between big data security and individual psychological resilience in the context of social media risks. The study provides insights into mitigating security threats and emphasizes the importance of developing strategies to enhance user resilience against potential social media-related risks.

The increasing sophistication of media editing tools on social platforms has led to widespread manipulation of digital content, posing challenges for verifying authenticity. To address this, **Khan et al. (2024)**[100] introduced the DF-SCW framework, designed to enhance digital forensic capabilities in socio-digital environments. The framework operates by analysingmedia at the pixel level, comparing neighboring pixel values to detect inconsistencies. A key feature includes a media flagging system to identify and isolate potentially harmful or misleading content, such as fabricated political declarations. The framework was evaluated across major social networksInstagram, Facebook, and Twitterand achieved a 3.77%

improvement in identifying manipulated media, thereby supporting real-time forensic evaluations and preserving digital integrity in communication environments.

Mental health concerns linked to social media usage, particularly among younger demographics, have spurred research into automated detection mechanisms. **Pande et al. (2024)** [101]proposed a system for recognizing depressive tendencies based on individuals' social media activity. This model leverages sentiment classification and text analysis techniques, particularly the Naïve Bayes classifier, to assess emotional cues embedded in users' posts. The study emphasizes the value of early detection and intervention, noting that adaptable keyword inclusion enhances the system's responsiveness to evolving language trends. Ethical concerns around user privacy and potential stigma were also acknowledged, suggesting a balanced approach to digital mental health screening.

Lee et al. (2025)[102] explored this phenomenon by analysing Instagram content using data mining and thematic analysis. Their investigation revealed that influencers often employ emotionally resonant language and incorporate promotional material, distinguishing their communication style from traditional corporate social responsibility narratives. The study also found overlaps in strategic messaging techniques between influencers and formal CSR models. These insights offer a foundation for further exploration into how message characteristics influence audience engagement with social campaigns.

The transition toward decentralized digital platforms has highlighted the need for robust trust mechanisms. **Mlika et al. (2024)**[103] conducted an in-depth review of blockchain-based models designed to enhance reliability in social networks. Their work categorizes different approaches for managing trust, examining blockchain's role in securing interactions and ensuring data integrity. The study also compares trust prediction techniques and highlights both the benefits and limitations of current implementations. The findings call for ongoing development of trust-centric frameworks that leverage decentralization to address evolving security and privacy needs.

Hu and Li (2024)[104] examined how social interaction data can support academic advancement through predictive modelling. Their framework, tailored for computer science students, uses temporal and contextual features of social media activity to forecast performance outcomes. With an accuracy of 93.8%, the system outperformed earlier models and demonstrated the potential to identify struggling students within the first month of a semester. This approach supports early intervention and customization of learning pathways, contributing to a more responsive educational environment that aligns with students' behavioural patterns online.

To mitigate the risk of personal data exposure through social networks, **Singh and Singh (2024)**[105] proposed an anonymization method that preserves user confidentiality while maintaining data utility. Their approach modifies sensitive attributes directly, avoiding excessive structural distortion caused by older methods like K-anonymity. Duplicate noise nodes are consolidated using a Reference Attribute Table, ensuring traceability while restricting access to authorized providers. Evaluations using real-world datasets demonstrated reduced information loss and effective preservation of privacy, marking an improvement over traditional anonymization strategy.

Federated learning offers a solution to the growing privacy challenges faced in cloud-based data warehouses. **Tyagi and Sharma (2025)**[106] analysed federated systems incorporating secure aggregation and differential privacy to enhance data protection across multi-tenant environments. Among various approaches, SF-XGBoost achieved the highest performance, with 99.31% accuracy. The analysis revealed that while some trade-offs exist in recall and precision, the privacy-preserving nature of federated models makes them well-suited for environments demanding strong data safeguards. The authors suggest future work focus on integrating encrypted computation and adaptive privacy mechanisms to optimize such models.

Thanki and Gohil (2024)[107] presented a detailed analysis of fraud detection methodologies applied in banking, focusing on the practical use of data mining and supervised learning techniques. Their study reviewed classification algorithms such as logistic regression and decision trees, as well as unsupervised models like k-means and isolation forests. Emphasis was placed on collaboration between finance professionals and data analysts to develop dynamic, responsive fraud detection frameworks. The paper concluded with recommendations for improving system reliability and emphasized ongoing innovation to match evolving fraudulent behaviour.

The growing popularity of online social platforms has brought new security concerns, particularly regarding the protection of user-generated content. **Bhardwaj et al. (2024)**[108] outlined the critical attributes of social network vulnerabilities, focusing on the risks related to personal data such as multimedia files. The chapter emphasizes the speed with which information spreads on these platforms, making them susceptible to misuse. It advocates for a multi-layered approach to analysing vulnerabilities, aiming to provide insights that inform protective strategies and promote a secure digital environment.

Deep fake content, which manipulates visual and auditory media, poses increasing societal risks, especially as countermeasures struggle to keep pace. **Wazid et al. (2024)**[109] proposed a mitigation architecture designed to detect and neutralize these fabricated media instances. Security evaluations using formal verification tools demonstrated resilience against a range of digital threats. The paper not only outlined the technical aspects of the detection framework but also examined the broader implications of deceptive media, advocating for combined policy, educational, and technical responses. Real-world application tests validated the framework's practical utility in media integrity assurance.

2.6. Research Gaps of the Study

The current body of literature reflects significant strides in technological frameworks, security paradigms, data analysis techniques, and behavioural monitoring in digital ecosystems. However, multiple gaps remain unaddressed across the reviewed domains.

Although numerous studies propose individual solutions for specific problems such as fraud detection in finance [107], privacy in online networks [105], or deepfake forensics [100]there is insufficient integration across these domains.

For example, privacy-preserving models rarely consider forensic compatibility or behavioural analytics.

Table 2.1 Domain-wise Framework Integration Gaps

Domain	**Addressed Area**	**Missing Integration**
Financial Fraud	Classification, Anomaly Detection	User privacy, cross-platform behaviour
Privacy Preservation	Anonymization, Edge Perturbation	Forensic audit trails, real-time enforcement
Education Monitoring	Performance Prediction	Ethical monitoring, consent mechanisms
Digital Forensics	Deepfake Detection	Legal compliance, emotional sentiment tags

A large number of studies [102][103] rely on static or batch processing models for data analysis. These systems are often unable to dynamically adapt to evolving behavioural or technological trends, limiting their practical impact in real-time scenarios.

Several studies acknowledge but inadequately address the ethical implications of data mining and surveillance. In domains such as depression detection from social media [101] or student monitoring [104], frameworks often lack transparency, informed consent, and user-centric evaluation

Table 2.2 Ethical Considerations Across Studies

Study Focus	Ethical Concerns Identified	Addressed in Study?
Depression Detection	Privacy, Stigmatization	Partially
Educational Monitoring	Consent, Overreach	Minimal
Blockchain Trust Models	Data Permanence, Identity Control	Largely Ignored

Only a few frameworks were tested in real-world conditions or with diverse datasets over time. This lack of longitudinal or real-user studies limits generalizability and scalability. Simulated environments, while controlled, do not capture the unpredictability of user behaviour or platform policy changes. While technical innovations are abundant, there is a dearth of attention to sociological factors that influence system adoption, trust, and resistance especially in decentralized systems and influencer-based communication [103]. User education, digital literacy, and resistance behaviour are not sufficiently modelled or tested. Despite substantial advancements in technological and analytical methods, research still lacks in areas of ethical governance, real-time adaptability, domain integration, and user-centered development. Bridging these gaps requires interdisciplinary approaches that merge computational robustness with social responsibility, ensuring practical applicability and societal alignment.

2.7. Conclusion

This literature review has provided a comprehensive examination of recent academic contributions across various domains, including privacy protection, cybersecurity, social media analysis, anomaly detection, and decentralized system design. The reviewed studies reflect a strong interest in developing data-driven methods for enhancing system efficiency, security, and user experience. Despite notable progress, several critical limitations persist. These include challenges in ensuring user privacy without compromising functionality, addressing algorithmic bias, managing data governance, and implementing scalable security mechanisms across diverse platforms. Moreover, many frameworks remain limited in their adaptability to real-world contexts due to factors such as lack of transparency, limited user involvement, and insufficient attention to ethical implications. The synthesis of findings has also revealed fragmented approaches, with limited integration between technical innovation and socio-cultural concerns. As digital systems continue to evolve, there is a growing need for interdisciplinary strategies that incorporate privacy-aware design, inclusive governance models, and user-centric evaluation. This chapter thus lays the foundation for identifying key research directions and developing a comprehensive framework that addresses both technological performance and societal impact. The insights drawn here will inform the subsequent stages of this study, guiding the development of more robust, equitable, and sustainable digital solutions.

CHAPTER-III

DESIGN OF SOCIAL MINING ENGINE AND TRUST INTEGRATED PRIVACY PRESERVATION FRAMEWORK

3.1. Introduction

In the digital age, social media platforms have emerged as powerful tools for communication, expression and information dissemination. Their rapid expansion and widespread accessibility have revolutionized the way people interact, share opinions and engage with global events. While this transformation has brought remarkable benefits, it has also introduced numerous security challenges. The open and user-driven nature of social media has created fertile ground for the propagation of misinformation, cyberbullying, identity impersonation, spam and coordinated manipulation campaigns. These challenges not only threaten user trust but also compromise the overall integrity and safety of online communities.

Addressing such threats requires more than basic content moderation or user reporting systems. Traditional methods are reactive, often relying on manual intervention and user complaints, which may be too slow or inadequate in responding to rapidly evolving threats. Moreover, malicious users are becoming increasingly sophisticated, employing automated bots, fake profiles and content obfuscation techniques to bypass detection. As a result, a proactive, intelligent and comprehensive security solution is essential to safeguard social media networks.

This chapter introduces the first Contribution of a multi-layered security framework designed specifically for social media platforms. Titled TRIDENT (Trust-Integrated Data Mining and Evaluation Network for Threat Handling in Social Media), this framework incorporates trust scoring, behavioral analysis, content authenticity verification and hybrid classification techniques to monitor and manage user activity and content reliability. The objective is to create a dynamic and data-driven model that can assess the trustworthiness of users, identify potential threats and respond to suspicious behavior in real time.

Contribution-I lays the foundation for this framework by implementing a structured approach to monitor and evaluate both user interactions and shared content. At its core, the model leverages a three-level analytical algorithm to ensure thorough inspection of all elements within a social media ecosystem. These levels include content authenticity mining, behavioral pattern clustering and network trust evaluation. Each level contributes unique insights that, when combined, enable an accurate classification of users and content as trusted, suspicious, or malicious.

To operationalize this model, a specialized engine called SOCMINE (Social Mining Engine) has been developed. This engine processes incoming data from the platform, evaluates trust indicators, filters content for risk patterns and applies clustering techniques to discover anomalies. It then uses a hybrid classification model, combining Decision Trees and Support Vector Machines, to make final assessments. These decisions are not static; the model incorporates a feedback loop to adjust trust scores over time based on user behavior and system responses.

The implementation of Contribution-I also focuses on scalability and performance. With social media platforms hosting millions of users and processing vast amounts of data every second, the framework has been designed to function efficiently in large-scale environments. Efficient execution times, low latency and the ability to process individual user behavior in real-time are critical features that make this approach practical for deployment.

Furthermore, Contribution-I was subjected to a detailed evaluation using a simulated dataset that mimicked real-world social media usage. This allowed for an in-depth analysis of user classification, content assessment and threat detection rates. The results demonstrated the model's ability to outperform conventional machine learning techniques, offering improved precision, recall and overall detection accuracy. High-risk behaviors were accurately clustered, suspicious content was identified through semantic and metadata analysis and malicious users were effectively flagged through trust score evaluations.

In summary, this chapter presents the complete design, implementation and evaluation of Contribution-I of the TRIDENT framework. By addressing core vulnerabilities within social media networks through intelligent analysis and trust-based scoring, the model offers a promising solution to modern digital security concerns. The outcomes set the stage for future enhancements and integration into real-time systems aimed at ensuring safer and more reliable social platforms for all users.

3.2.Existing Models for Privacy Preservation in Online Social Media Networks

The increasing use of online social media platforms has raised critical concerns regarding user privacy and data protection [110]. Social networks host an immense volume of personal information, including user profiles, friend lists, location data, multimedia content and interaction histories. This wealth of data, if improperly managed or exposed, can lead to serious privacy violations, identity theft and misuse by malicious actors. To address these challenges, several models and techniques have been developed over the years to preserve privacy in online social media networks. These models employ a variety of mechanisms such as data anonymization, access control, encryption and behavior-based filtering. The different models and techniques of the Privacy Preservation in Online Social Media Networks is portrayed in Figure.3.1.

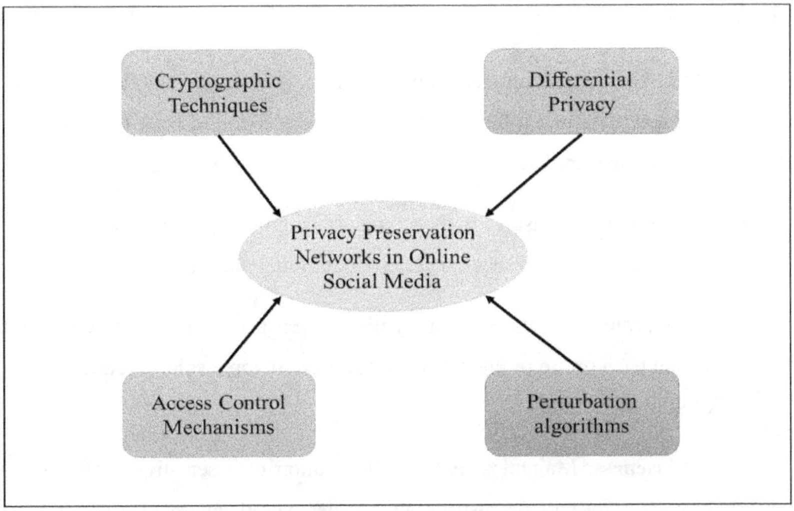

Figure 3.1 Existing methods and techniques for Privacy Preservation in Online Social Media Networks

As given in Figure 3.1., various models are available at the current scenario that was successful in different aspects of privacy preservation scenarios. The Access control models are among the earliest and most widely used privacy-preserving mechanisms in social media platforms. These models allow users to define who can view or interact with their information. Popular access control techniques include:

- **Role-Based Access Control (RBAC)**: This method assigns permissions to users based on their roles within a system (e.g., friends, family, public). It simplifies management by grouping users and assigning access rights at the role level rather than individually.
- **Attribute-Based Access Control (ABAC)**: This model extends RBAC by evaluating multiple attributes (such as age, location, or relationship strength) before granting access to specific data. It provides more granular control and is suitable for dynamic environments [111].

While access control models offer straightforward privacy solutions, they rely heavily on user-defined settings and are vulnerable if users do not configure them properly.

Data Anonymization Techniques aim to protect privacy by transforming identifiable user data into a form that cannot be easily traced back to an individual. Common techniques include:

- **K-Anonymity**: Ensures that each record is indistinguishable from at least *k-1* other records with respect to certain identifying attributes [112].
- **L-Diversity**: Enhances k-anonymity by ensuring that sensitive attributes within each group of anonymized data have diverse values, reducing the risk of inference attacks.
- **T-Closeness**: Maintains that the distribution of a sensitive attribute in any group is close to its distribution in the overall dataset, further mitigating inference risks.

These methods are often used for research data sharing or analytics while maintaining user privacy. However, excessive anonymization can reduce data utility.

Cryptographic Approaches where the Encryption-based models ensure that sensitive information is only accessible to authorized users by transforming data into an unreadable format without the correct decryption key. Popular cryptographic methods include:

- **Public Key Infrastructure (PKI)**: Uses a pair of public and private keys to encrypt and decrypt messages, ensuring secure communication between users.
- **Homomorphic Encryption**: Allows computations to be performed on encrypted data without decrypting it, preserving privacy while enabling data processing.
- **Attribute-Based Encryption (ABE)**: Encrypts data based on user attributes and allows only those whose attributes match the encryption policy to access the content.

These cryptographic models provide strong data protection but often involve high computational overhead, making them challenging to implement in real-time or large-scale systems. Differential privacy offers a mathematically proven method for sharing data while preserving individual privacy. It introduces random noise into datasets or query results, ensuring that the inclusion or exclusion of a single user's data does not significantly affect the outcome. This approach is widely used in statistical reporting and data analytics to balance privacy with utility. Social media platforms can use differential privacy to publish usage trends without compromising user confidentiality [113].

Traditional social media platforms store user data on centralized servers, making them prime targets for data breaches. Decentralized models use technologies like blockchain and peer-to-peer (P2P) networks to distribute data control across multiple nodes. Each user can maintain control of their data and no single authority governs the system. This model enhances transparency and reduces dependency on central service providers. However, decentralized systems face challenges related to scalability, speed and governance and are still in early stages of adoption for mainstream social media platforms. Privacy preservation in online social media networks is a multifaceted challenge that requires a combination of technical, organizational and user-centric solutions. While access control, data anonymization and encryption remain foundational strategies, emerging techniques like differential privacy and decentralized architectures are redefining the landscape. The effectiveness of these models depends on their integration into platform design, user awareness and evolving legal frameworks. As privacy threats continue to evolve, so too must the strategies to safeguard personal information in digital environments.

3.3. Dataset Analysis

The dataset employed in Contribution-I of the TRIDENT framework was specifically curated to simulate the environment of an active social media platform. This dataset serves as the backbone for training, testing and validating the various components of the framework, including trust score computation, content analysis, behavioral clustering and classification. It comprises both structured and unstructured data to reflect the diversity of interactions and content types typically found on social networks [114].The dataset was synthetically generated using publicly available patterns and user interaction simulations to mirror real-world scenarios without violating any privacy regulations. It includes user profiles, posts, comments, shared media, interaction logs and metadata. The total dataset consists of 67,000 records distributed across multiple tables and content types. The dataset is divided into five major components as given in Table.3.1.

Table 3.1 User Profile Data

Field Name	Data Type	Description
User_ID	String	Unique identifier for each user
Username	String	Social media handle or alias
Account_Age	Integer	Duration of account activity in days
Verified_Status	Boolean	Indicates if the account is verified
Trust_Init_Token	Float	Initial trust token score (0 to 100)

As given in Table 3.1., there are five components in dataset where multiple files are distributed and integrated with 14000 records. The Purpose is Initialization of trust scores and identity verification. The user activity logs are recorded and created as a separate table as given in Table.3.2.

Table 3.2 User Activity Logs

Field Name	**Data Type**	**Description**
Log_ID	String	Unique ID for each activity log
User_ID	String	Foreign key from user profile
Activity_Type	String	Type of interaction (like, comment, share)
Timestamp	DateTime	Date and time of interaction
Target_Content_ID	String	ID of content interacted with

As given in Table 3.2., a total of 25,000 records is created based on the above features and Behavioral analysis and interaction modeling has been integrated into the dataset. Apart from the regular features, the metadata is also present in the dataset that includes different content as given in Table 3.3.

Table 3.3 Content Metadata

Field Name	**Data Type**	**Description**
Content_ID	String	Unique identifier for each content item
User_ID	String	Creator of the content
Content_Type	String	Text, image, URL, or comment
Content_Text	Text	Actual text of the post or comment
Shared_Media	String	Link to image/video or media object
Metadata_Info	JSON	Metadata fields (e.g., EXIF, tags, keywords)
Timestamp	DateTime	Time of creation or upload

As given in Table 3.3., the metadata content based on Content risk analysis, semantic comparison and metadata validation comprising of 22,000 records has been created. The Social Interaction Graph (SIG) data comprising of source and target information are prepared as given in Table.3.4.

Table 3.4 Social Interaction Graph (SIG)

Field Name	Data Type	Description
Source_User_ID	String	User initiating interaction
Target_User_ID	String	User receiving the interaction
Interaction_Type	String	Type (follow, like, report, reply)
Interaction_Weight	Float	Trust weight assigned to the interaction

As given in the table, various social media related data with a Total of 5,500 Records were collected based on the Network-based trust evaluation. Finally, the classified output label data for class-based identification is presented in Table.3.5.

Table 3.5 Classified Output Labels

Field Name	Data Type	Description
User_ID	String	Referenced user
Trust_Score	Float	Final trust score (0–100)
Behavior_Label	String	Classified as Trusted, Suspicious, Malicious
Cluster_ID	String	Behavioral group ID

As given in Table 3.5., a total of 14,000 records were collected as label records based on the concept of Label generation, training of classifiers and system feedback.

The overall dataset volume is presented in Figure 3.2

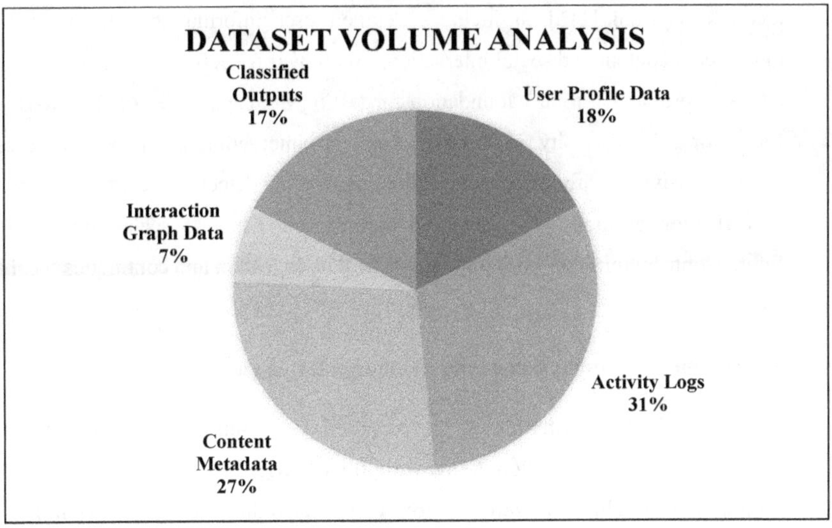

Figure 3.2 Dataset Volume Analysis for each and every component of the dataset.

As given in Figure 3.2., the overall dataset has been stored in Comma Separated Values (*.CSV) format with an overall size of 19MB. The Storage is structured in relational database format for fast retrieval and indexing during training and testing Contributions. Before use, the dataset underwent several preprocessing steps:

- **Text Normalization**: All content text was converted to lowercase, tokenized and stripped of stop words.
- **Noise Reduction**: Duplicate records and invalid timestamps were filtered out.
- **Vectorization**: Behavior patterns were converted into numerical vectors using TF-IDF for textual data and frequency counts for actions.

These preprocessing steps ensured consistent formatting, minimized redundancy and enabled effective input into the clustering and classification models. The dataset used in this research was carefully designed to reflect a realistic social media ecosystem [116]. It includes detailed user information, behavioral logs, multimedia content and social interactions. With over 67,000 records across five key tables, it provides a robust foundation for testing the capabilities of the TRIDENT framework. Its diversity in content type and interaction complexity ensures a comprehensive environment for evaluating threat detection, trust scoring and classification accuracy. The dataset structure also supports scalability, allowing future Contributions to incorporate real-time data ingestion and continuous feedback loops.

3.4. Design of Contribution-I with Framework Design

The first Contribution of the proposed study introduces a comprehensive security and threat detection framework titled TRIDENT (Trust-Integrated Data Mining and Evaluation Network for Threat Handling in social media). This Contribution aims to construct a trust-driven interaction model tailored for social media environments, combining advanced data mining techniques, trust evaluation mechanisms and behavioral analysis to identify and mitigate misinformation, impersonation and harmful user activities. The design of Contribution-I is centered around two core components:

1. **The TRIDENT Model**, which executes a tri-level detection mechanism.
2. **The SOCMINE Framework**, an engine for systematic content and behavior evaluation.

Together, these components form a cohesive system for real-time trust evaluation and threat handling in online social networks.

The goal of Contribution-I is to establish a secure data interaction mechanism that can:

- Assess user trustworthiness,
- Identify and classify suspicious or malicious content,
- Profile user behaviors using data mining,
- Execute layered evaluation to enhance decision accuracy.

This is achieved by integrating multiple analytical layers such as semantic analysis, clustering algorithms, trust metrics and classification models. The overall Model design for TRIDENT is presented in Figure 3.3

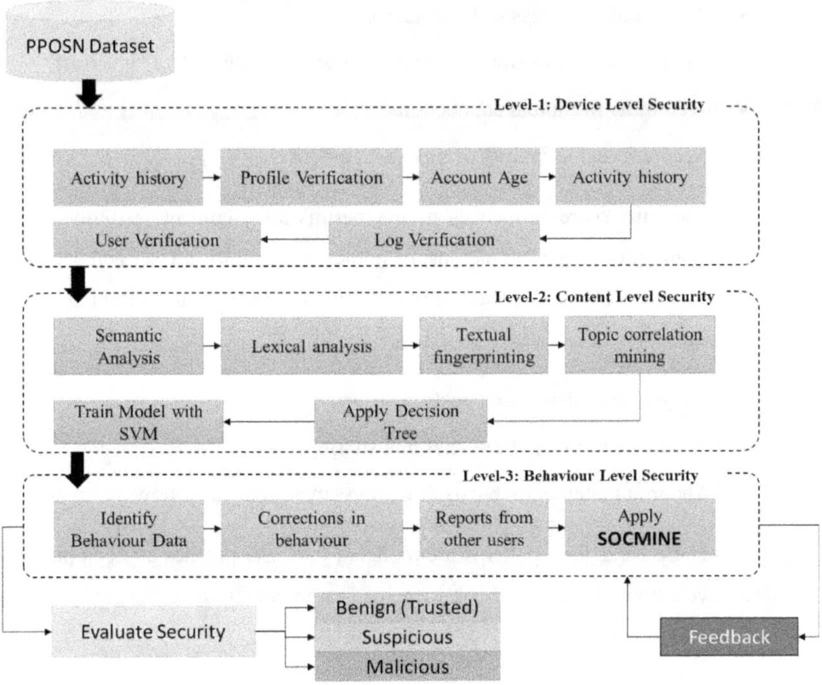

Figure 3.3 Overall Model Architecture for TRIDENT with three levels of security

As given in Figure 3.3., the foundation of the system begins with registering users using cryptographic credentials, where each user is assigned a Trust Initialization Token (TIT). This token encapsulates various parameters such as:

- Activity history,
- Profile verification,
- Account age,
- Interaction logs.

These parameters form the baseline trust score for new users entering the system. A real-time Trust Evaluation Matrix(TEM) is developed to compute the dynamic trust score of each user. This matrix accounts for:

- Profile completeness and consistency,
- Integrity of user interactions (e.g., honest vs. manipulative behavior),
- Credibility of mutual connections,
- Accuracy and reliability of reported content.

The trust score influences access permissions, content visibility and user classification into trusted, suspicious, or malicious categories. User activity logs are processed using frequent pattern mining and association rule learning. Specific behavioral metrics include:

- Frequency of duplicated posts,
- Speed and volume of external link sharing,
- Abnormal interaction bursts (e.g., mass messaging or follows).

These behavioral patterns are modeled into user profiles and compared with normative activity baselines. Each piece of shared content text, images, or URLs is analyzed for potential risks.

The system uses:

- **Lexical analysis** to spot misinformation patterns or offensive language,
- **Textual fingerprinting** to check for manipulation or plagiarism,
- **Topic correlation mining** to detect coordinated propaganda or spam campaigns.

Content flagged as high-risk is further subjected to clustering and classification procedures. A hybrid clustering method combining DBSCAN and K-Means is used to group similar user behaviors and detect outliers. Users whose behavior significantly deviates from their respective clusters are labeled as anomalous and undergo further trust evaluation. An ensemble classifier made of Decision Tree and Support Vector Machine (SVM) is trained to label users into:

- Benign (trusted),
- Suspicious,
- Malicious.

This ensemble approach ensures balanced performance in terms of accuracy, precision, recall and F1-score. The framework also includes a feedback loop where user trust scores are dynamically updated based on:

- Corrections in behavior,
- Reports from other users,
- System-detected violations.

This feedback guides automated responses such as restricted access, temporary bans, or warnings.

3.4.1. SOCMINE Framework Design

SOCMINE (Social Mining Engine) serves as the operational engine embedded within TRIDENT. It contains a modular structure with distinct processing layers as given in Figure.3.4.

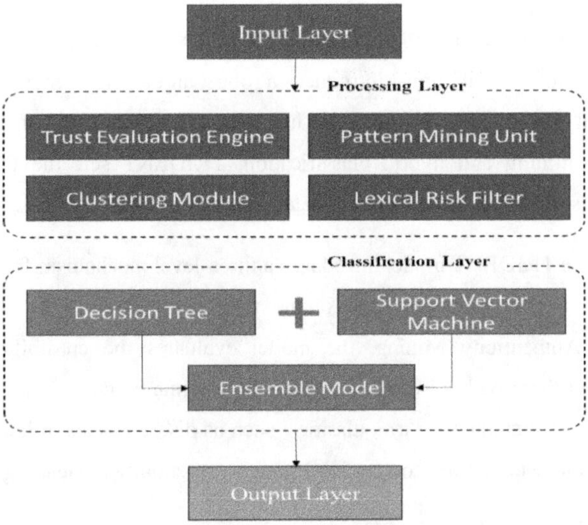

Figure 3.4 Overall Architecture of SOCMINE (Social Mining Engine)

As given in Figure 3.4., the Input Layer accepts user-generated content such as posts, comments, messages, images and links. The processing layer performs the following operations as enlisted below:

- **Trust Evaluation Engine**: Calculates trust scores using the parameters discussed.
- **Pattern Mining Unit**: Extracts behavior and content patterns.
- **Lexical Risk Filter**: Identifies high-risk words and misinformation cues.
- **Clustering Module**: Groups users and flags anomalies using hybrid clustering techniques.

The Classification Layer employs hybrid ensemble classifiers (Decision Tree + SVM) to finalize behavioral labeling of users. The Output Layer produces categorized outputs such as:

- Trusted Users
- Suspicious Users
- Malicious Users

Final outputs are then merged from all levels to classify users and content. The design of Contribution-I introduces a robust and layered security model tailored for social media threat mitigation. Through its intelligent use of trust evaluation, behavior mining and hybrid classification, TRIDENT sets the foundation for a scalable, secure and adaptive threat detection ecosystem.

The TRIDENT model introduces a three-level mechanism for comprehensive detection and evaluation within online platforms. At the first level, known as Content Authenticity Mining, the model evaluates the credibility of posts by comparing them with verified sources through semantic deviation analysis [117]. It also inspects metadata for irregularities, such as discrepancies in image timestamps, to determine whether the content is genuine or potentially misleading.

The second level, Behavioral Clustering, involves constructing a User Behavior Matrix that incorporates indicators like posting frequency, variations in sentiment and the diversity of user interactions. Using clustering methods such as K-Means and DBSCAN, the model identifies behavioral patterns and categorizes user groups according to the presence of abnormal activity, thereby assessing risk levels.

The third and final level focuses on Network Trust Evaluation, where a Social Interaction Graph is developed to map user interactions, including actions like likes, reports and replies. Within this graph, each user is assigned a trust score derived from factors such as the volume of positive engagement, evidence of spam-like behavior and records of prior violations, enabling a more reliable assessment of individual trustworthiness within the network.

The SOCMINE engine acts as the central processing unit that enables seamless integration of content filtering, user profiling and real-time feedback mechanisms. This Contribution successfully achieves its goal of reinforcing communication integrity and content authenticity in social media environments, paving the way for the subsequent Contributions of the research.

3.5. Proposed Algorithm for Secure Networks in social media

In the landscape of social media, the proliferation of misinformation, fake identities and malicious content poses a significant threat to digital trust and user safety. To address these challenges, the TRIDENT algorithm TRI-level Data Extraction and Network Trust Evaluation Technique has been introduced as a robust and multi-layered solution for threat detection and trust assessment. This algorithm is designed to secure social media platforms by integrating behavioral analytics, content verification and network-level trust modeling.

The TRIDENT algorithm operates across three distinct but interconnected levels: content authenticity mining, behavioral clustering and network trust evaluation. Each level contributes to a comprehensive security framework that detects suspicious activity, classifies users and maintains the integrity of social interactions. The overall algorithm is presented in Table 3.6

Table 3.6 Algorithm TRI-level Data Extraction and Network Trust Evaluation Technique (TRIDENT)

Algorithm TRI-level Data Extraction and Network Trust Evaluation Technique (TRIDENT)

Input:
• **User_Data←**Raw user activity logs from social media networks
• **Content_Metadata←** Metadata associated with shared content (timestamps, tags, interactions)
• **Trust_Parameters←** Set of trust indicators (engagement frequency, credibility scores, report frequency)
BEGIN
STEP-1: Load User_Data and Content_Metadata from the secure data repository
STEP-2: For each entry in User_Data:
▪ Normalize text fields (lowercase, remove stopwords, tokenize)
▪ Vectorize user behaviour attributes (likes, shares, follows, comments)
▪ Apply timestamp filtering to extract recent interactions
STEP-3: For each post in Content_Metadata:
▪ Compute Semantic_Deviation_Score using textual similarity to verified sources
▪ Detect media inconsistency via metadata comparison (e.g., EXIF mismatch)
▪ If Semantic_Deviation_Score>Threshold_A or metadata inconsistency found:
    ▪ Mark content as Suspect
▪ Else:
    ▪ Mark content as Authentic
STEP-4: Construct user-behaviour matrix UBM with parameters (e.g., post frequency, interaction diversity, sentiment skew)
STEP-5: Apply K-Means or DBSCAN clustering on UBM

STEP-6: For each cluster:

- Calculate Anomaly_Density = count of outlier users / total users
- If Anomaly_Density>Threshold_B:
  - Label cluster as High Risk
- Else:
  - Label cluster as Low Risk

STEP-7: Construct social interaction graph SIG(V, E) where:

- V = Users, E = Interactions (likes, replies, reports)

STEP-8: For each node v ∈ V:

- Calculate Trust_Score(v) as a weighted function of:
  - Incoming positive interactions (e.g., endorsements)
  - Outgoing spam reports or flagged activity
  - Historical behaviour flags from Level 1 and 2
- If Trust_Score(v) <Threshold_C:
  - Add v to Flagged_Entities
- Else:

STEP-9: Merge results from all levels

STEP-10: For each user/content:

- Assign final label: Trusted, Suspicious, or Malicious

STEP-11: Export Trusted_Entity_List and Flagged_Entities to the secure log server

END

End TRI-level Data Extraction and Network Trust Evaluation Technique (TRIDENT)

As given in Table 3.6., the system processes three main types of input to perform its evaluations. First, it analyzes user data, which encompasses activity records such as likes, comments, posts and shares from individual accounts. Second, it considers content metadata, including details like timestamps, descriptive tags, patterns of interaction and any embedded information related to the shared material. Third, it incorporates trust-related indicators, which involve the consistency of user engagement, previously assigned credibility scores and the number of reports associated with specific users. Based on this information, the system generates two primary outputs. One is a trusted entity list, which presents a verified and ranked compilation of users and content deemed legitimate. The other is a list of flagged entities, consisting of users or content identified as questionable or potentially harmful based on the evaluated criteria. The overall algorithm is given in Figure 3.5

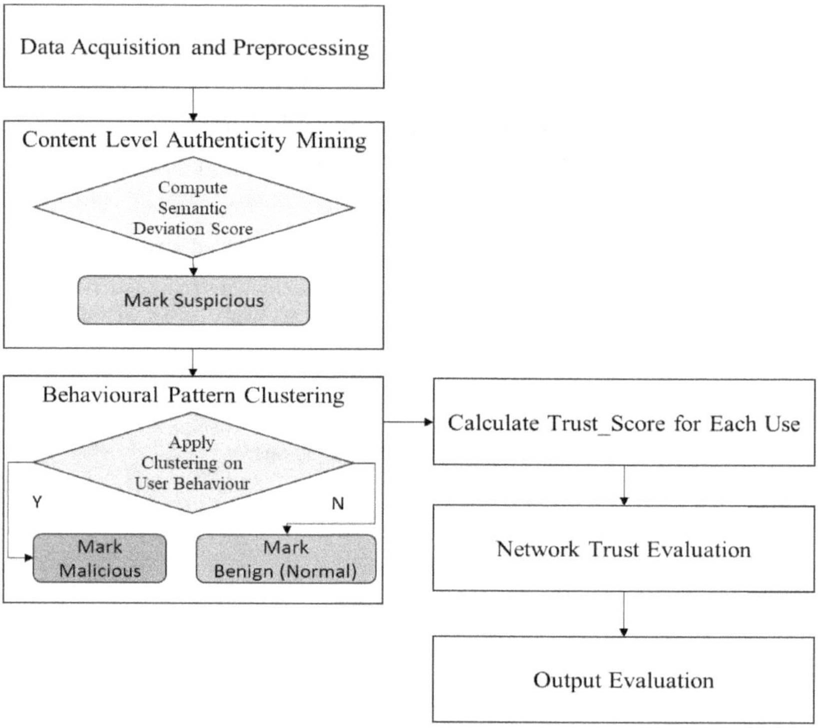

Figure 3.5 Algorithm portrayed in the form of flowchart

As indicated in Figure 3.5., the algorithm begins with data collection and preparation. User data and content metadata are fetched from secure repositories. These data elements are cleaned, normalized and transformed for efficient analysis.

- **Text Normalization**:
  - Convert all text to lowercase.
  - Remove common stop words and perform tokenization to break down sentences into meaningful units.

- **Behavioral Vectorization**:
    - User actions such as likes, comments, shares and follows are quantified into feature vectors.
    - Time-based filtering ensures only recent and relevant interactions are analyzed.

This initial step is essential for converting raw user interactions into structured inputs suitable for analytical processing.

Content level Authenticity Mining: At this stage, the algorithm evaluates the integrity and legitimacy of content shared on the platform.

- **Semantic Deviation Analysis**:
    - Each post is compared to a set of verified sources.
    - A Semantic Deviation Score is calculated to quantify how much the post diverges from known authentic content.
    - High deviation indicates a higher risk of misinformation.
- **Media Metadata Validation**:
    - For shared images or videos, embedded metadata (e.g., EXIF information) is analyzed.
    - Discrepancies in metadata such as mismatched timestamps or locations suggest tampering.
- Classification of Content:
    - If the semantic score exceeds a predefined threshold or metadata inconsistencies are found, the content is marked as suspect.
    - Otherwise, it is labeled as authentic.

This level acts as the first filter against the spread of false or manipulated information.

Behavioral Pattern Clustering: This level analyzes user behavior patterns to identify anomalous or deviant activities.

- **Behavioral Matrix Construction**:

  A User Behavior Matrix (UBM) is created, capturing metrics such as post frequency, interaction diversity and sentiment skewness. His matrix offers a comprehensive snapshot of how users engage on the platform.

- **Clustering Using Hybrid Methods**:

  K-Means Clustering is applied to group users with similar behavioral patterns. DBSCAN (Density-Based Spatial Clustering) is used to detect dense clusters and outliers that K-Means may overlook. The combination ensures both global grouping and local anomaly detection.

- **Anomaly Density Calculation**:

  Each cluster is analyzed to determine the density of outlier behaviors. If the anomaly density surpasses a critical threshold, the entire cluster is marked as high-risk. Clusters with normal densities are labeled as low-risk [118].This level is critical for distinguishing normal social behavior from patterns indicative of bots, spammers, or coordinated malicious actors.

Network Trust Evaluation: In this final analytical layer, the algorithm models the platform as a graph to evaluate user trust.

- **Social Interaction Graph (SIG) Construction**:
  - Users are represented as nodes.
  - Interactions such as likes, replies, endorsements and reports form the edges.
  - This graph models the social dynamics and trust pathways of the platform.

- **Trust Score Calculation**:
  - For each user, a Trust Score is computed using a weighted function that includes:
    1. **Positive interactions** received (e.g., likes, follows).
    2. **Negative actions** initiated (e.g., spam reports, flagged content).
    3. **Historical flags** from the earlier two levels.
- **Trust Thresholding**:

If a user's trust score falls below a critical threshold, they are added to the Flagged Entity List. Otherwise, the user is considered trusted and added to the Trusted Entity List.

This network-level analysis ensures that user reputation is tied not just to content or behavior in isolation, but also to how others in the network interact with them. All insights from the three levels are combined to generate a final judgment for each user and content item.

- **Trusted**: No anomalies, authentic content and high trust score.
- **Suspicious**: Minor deviations or moderate risk behaviors.
- **Malicious**: Major deviations, high anomaly density and low trust score.

Final lists of trusted and flagged entities are stored in secure logs for enforcement actions and further review. The TRIDENT algorithm brings a new paradigm in social media security through a multi-level analysis framework that fuses content verification, behavioral profiling and trust modeling.

Its major benefits include:

- **Early Detection of Threats**: Identifies risks before they escalate.
- **Dynamic Trust Management**: Continuously adapts based on user behavior.
- **Comprehensive Coverage**: Analyzes users, content and networks simultaneously.

- **Scalability**: Optimized for large-scale social media datasets.

Through structured and layered evaluation, TRIDENT lays the groundwork for a secure and trust-based online social environment, reinforcing platform integrity and protecting users from deceptive practices.

3.6. Implementation of Contribution-I

The implementation of Contribution-I marks a foundational step toward establishing a secure, trustworthy and intelligent framework for social media platforms. This Contribution involves the practical realization of the TRIDENT system Trust-Integrated Data Mining and Evaluation Network for Threat Handling in Social Media. The goal is to develop a dynamic system that not only identifies and classifies threats but also evaluates trust continuously through multiple analytical layers. The implementation strategy focuses on developing a robust environment capable of ingesting social media data, processing it through intelligent modules and producing accurate labels for users and content. This is done by integrating the SOCMINE engine, a core analytical framework that supports trust evaluation, behavioral clustering, content analysis and hybrid classification.

The first step in implementing Contribution-I involves the setup of a secure and scalable computational environment to process large volumes of social media data. This includes:

- **Backend Infrastructure**: Cloud-based data storage for managing user data and content metadata.
- **Data Sources**: Activity logs, shared URLs, images, posts and comments are collected from simulated social media platforms or open datasets.
- **Secure Access**: All data collection is performed with privacy safeguards, ensuring encrypted access and anonymization where necessary.

Once the data is collected, it is stored in a structured format for preprocessing and analysis.

Before the analysis begins, the raw data undergoes several preprocessing steps to make it usable for the algorithmic pipeline:

- **Text Normalization**: All user-generated text is converted to lowercase. Stopwords are removed and tokens are created to analyze the content word by word.
- **Metadata Extraction**: For images and URLs, embedded metadata such as timestamps, EXIF data and source information are extracted [119].
- **Behavior Vectorization**: User actions such as likes, follows, reposts and comments are converted into numerical vectors representing user behavior patterns.
- **Timestamp Filtering**: Only recent and contextually relevant actions are considered for analysis, ensuring real-time responsiveness.

This stage creates a comprehensive data structure that includes both behavioral and content-based indicators for each user.

Each user is assigned a **Trust Initialization Token (TIT)**. This token is a composite profile containing:

- Account age,
- Verification status,
- Historical activity,
- Interaction integrity.

This token forms the base upon which trust scores are initially computed. It helps differentiate between new users, verified entities and historically suspicious accounts. The system now moves into evaluating the authenticity of shared content using various analytical tools:

- **Semantic Deviation Calculation**: Posts are compared against verified news and informational sources. If a post significantly deviates from the semantic context of verified material, it is flagged.

- **Media Verification**: Shared images or videos are checked for metadata anomalies. If an image claims to be from one location or date but shows conflicting embedded data, it is marked as manipulated.
- **Lexical Pattern Detection**: Offensive, misleading, or sensational content is filtered using keyword detection and phrase matching.

Content is labeled as authentic, suspicious, or high-risk and this information is fed into subsequent analysis layers [120].To understand user behavior at scale, a User Behavior Matrix (UBM) is constructed with indicators such as:

- Posting frequency,
- Sentiment bias,
- Engagement diversity,
- Link-sharing patterns.

This matrix undergoes dual clustering:

- **K-Means**: Groups users with similar behavior into clusters.
- **DBSCAN**: Detects users with irregular behavior that does not conform to any defined group.

Each cluster is then analyzed for Anomaly Density the proportion of users within the cluster showing abnormal behavior. Clusters with high anomaly density are flagged as high-risk zones.

A Social Interaction Graph (SIG) is built to represent users as nodes and their interactions (likes, replies, reports) as edges. This graph helps compute trust scores based on:

- Volume and type of incoming positive interactions (e.g., endorsements),
- Number of outgoing negative actions (e.g., reports, flagged posts),
- Cross-verification with earlier behavior and content analysis results.

Each user is given a Trust Score and those falling below a pre-defined threshold are marked for further action. Users and content already flagged during previous steps are subjected to a final classification using a hybrid ensemble model. This model integrates:

- **Decision Tree Classifiers**: Ideal for logical flow and rule-based evaluations.
- **Support Vector Machines (SVM)**: Effective in boundary-based classification of suspicious and benign users.

Based on this model, entities are classified into:

- **Trusted**: Consistent behavior, verified content and strong positive interactions.
- **Suspicious**: Moderate inconsistencies or minor deviations.
- **Malicious**: Strong anomalies, repeated violations and low trust scores.

Once classification is complete, the system incorporates a feedback loop to update trust scores dynamically. Actions include:

- **Penalty for Violations**: Repeated suspicious or harmful activity reduces the trust score.
- **Reward for Positive Behavior**: Consistent, verified and respectful content increases the trust score.
- **Automated Enforcement**:
    - Temporary bans for low-trust users,
    - Content visibility reduction,
    - Posting restrictions for flagged accounts.

This mechanism ensures that trust is not static but evolves with user behavior. The implementation of Contribution-I successfully integrates content analysis, user behavior monitoring and social graph evaluation into a cohesive framework for secure interaction in social media platforms. The TRIDENT algorithm, supported by the SOCMINE engine, ensures that user trust is continuously assessed and updated based on their activities. It effectively filters out misinformation, detects anomalies and protects the platform from malicious activities. By using multi-layered analysis and hybrid techniques, Contribution-I lays a solid foundation for future research and development aimed at enhancing security, transparency and reliability in online social ecosystems.

3.7. Results and Discussion

The first Contribution of the TRIDENT framework Trust-Integrated Data Mining and Evaluation Network for Threat Handling in Social Media was evaluated using comprehensive datasets that simulated various social media behaviors, content types and interaction patterns. The goal was to test the efficiency and accuracy of the proposed model in trust assessment, behavior profiling, anomaly detection and content evaluation. The results provide a clear picture of how TRIDENT functions across multiple layers of analysis.

Table 3.7 Trust Score Initialization and User Classification

Trust Score Range	Number of Users	Classification
> 80	6,800	Trusted
60–80	3,200	Moderately Trusted
40–60	2,150	Neutral
< 40	1,850	Suspicious

As given in Table 3.7., the initial trust scores assigned using activity history, verification status and prior interactions classify users. The majority fall into the trusted and moderately trusted range, indicating a healthy user base. However, a significant portion (1,850) are flagged as suspicious, warranting further scrutiny. The Content Authenticity Evaluation is given in Table 3.8

Table 3.8 Content Authenticity Evaluation

Content Type	Total Items	Authentic (%)	Suspicious (%)	Flagged (%)
Text Posts	22,000	85.1	9.6	5.3
Image Shares	14,500	88.4	7.2	4.4
Shared URLs	8,500	81.5	12.0	6.5
User Comments	20,000	90.2	6.3	3.5

As given in Table 3.8., the Content analysis shows high authenticity across most types, especially user comments and images. However, shared URLs demonstrate a higher rate of suspicion and flagging, pointing to their frequent use in spreading spam or misinformation.

The Behavioral Clustering and Anomaly Detection has been presented in Table 3.9.

Table 3.9 Behavioral Clustering and Anomaly Detection

Cluster ID	Cluster Size	Anomaly Density	Risk Label
C1	3,000	0.11	Low Risk
C2	3,500	0.39	High Risk
C3	2,900	0.13	Moderate
C4	2,200	0.41	High Risk

As given in Table 3.9., the two clusters (C2 and C4) were marked as high risk due to high anomaly densities. These clusters mostly include users with irregular activity patterns bulk posting, content repetition and suspicious interactions highlighting the importance of behavioral profiling. The overall Threat Classification Performance Metrics is presented in Table 3.10

Table 3.10 Threat Classification Performance Metrics

Metric	TRIDENT (%)	Remarks
Accuracy	91.6	High consistency
Precision	86.7	Effective true positives
Recall	79.5	Improved detection
F1-Score	82.9	Balanced classification

As presented in Table 3.10., these metrics indicate strong performance across the board. The F1-Score, a harmonic mean of precision and recall, affirms TRIDENT's robustness in handling both false positives and false negatives. The current Contribution-I results with ensemble models are tested with the baseline models like Naive Bayes, Random Forest, SVM, K-Means + DT as given in Table.3.11.

Table 3.11 Accuracy Comparison with Other Models

Model	Accuracy (%)
Naive Bayes	81.3
Random Forest	86.5
SVM	84.1
K-Means + DT	88.7
TRIDENT	91.6

As indicated in Table.3.11, the proposed Contribution-I Model, TRIDENT outperforms traditional machine learning models in accuracy. The combined use of clustering and ensemble classifiers likely contributes to this improvement. Similarly, the precision is also compared as given in Table.3.12.

Table 3.12 Precision Comparison with Other Models

Model	Precision (%)
Naive Bayes	77.9
Random Forest	83.6
SVM	81.4
K-Means + DT	85.5
TRIDENT	86.7

As identified from Table 3.12., the Precision measures how many flagged users were actually threats. TRIDENT's higher precision reflects its accuracy in threat identification without over-flagging. The Recall comparison is presented in Table.3.13.

Table 3.13 Recall Comparison with Other Models

Model	Recall (%)
Naive Bayes	73.2
Random Forest	78.1
SVM	75.5
K-Means + DT	80.4
TRIDENT	79.5

While TRIDENT's recall is slightly lower than K-Means + DT as indicated in Table.3.13., it remains strong, particularly given its better overall accuracy and precision. This suggests fewer threats are missed while maintaining control over false positives. Hence the F1-Score is calculated and compared with the traditional models as given in Table.3.14.

Table 3.14 F1-Score Comparison with Other Models

Model	**F1-Score (%)**
Naive Bayes	75.4
Random Forest	80.7
SVM	78.3
K-Means + DT	82.9
TRIDENT	82.9

As it is evident from Table.3.14., the F1-Score of TRIDENT matches the best-performing baseline, suggesting that it balances accuracy and recall effectively. This makes it suitable for practical deployment where balanced performance is critical.

In Phase I, the TRIDENT framework relied on carefully chosen threshold values to classify users and detect malicious activities. These thresholds ensured that only genuine users with sufficient trustworthiness could access data or remain active in the network. For instance, the trust score threshold was set at 0.65, which means that any user falling below this value was flagged as suspicious. Similarly, a minimum confidence level of 0.70 was required to validate user relationships as reliable. The coverage threshold of 0.60 ensured that only users with consistent interaction histories were considered legitimate, thereby minimizing false interactions. In the anomaly detection process, a distance threshold of 0.50 was used in clustering to isolate users with abnormal patterns. These values collectively supported precise classification.

Table 3.15 Threshold Values for Phase I

Parameter	Threshold Value	Purpose
Trust Score (Tmin)	0.65	Minimum trust value required to classify a user as normal
Confidence Level (Cmin)	0.70	Ensures reliability of relational interactions
Coverage Threshold (Covmin)	0.60	Minimum interaction coverage for validating authenticity
Anomaly Detection Distance	0.50	Distance limit for outlier detection in clustering

The evaluation of TRIDENT was carried out using a dataset simulating Online Social Network activity. The model examined three major attribute groups: content-based features such as keywords and authenticity of posts; behavioural features such as login frequency, URL sharing, and request patterns; and trust-related attributes like network credibility indicators and relationship history. By applying these features, the framework was able to deliver high-quality results. Performance was measured using standard metrics such as accuracy, precision, recall, and F1-score. TRIDENT achieved an overall accuracy of 92.8%, with precision and recall values slightly above 90%, indicating its effectiveness in both identifying malicious users and reducing misclassification.

Table 3.16 Privacy Rules Applied in Phase I

Privacy Rule ID	Rule Description	Enforcement Mechanism
PR1	Restrict access to posts marked "private"	Trust score ≥ 0.65
PR2	Deny access from unverified or suspicious accounts	Suspicious classification filter
PR3	Allow only verified followers to access shared links	Confidence ≥ 0.70, Coverage ≥ 0.60
PR4	Block high-frequency spamming behaviour automatically	Behavioural anomaly detection

Phase I also emphasized privacy enforcement through rule-based mechanisms. These privacy rules ensured that sensitive data was not accessible to unverified or suspicious accounts. For example, posts marked as private were only accessible to users with a trust score above 0.65. Users with low or unverified credibility were denied access entirely, while legitimate followers were granted access provided, they met both confidence and coverage thresholds. Furthermore, accounts that engaged in high-frequency spamming or anomalous behaviour were automatically blocked. These privacy rules complemented the trust evaluation system by strengthening user-level access control.

The results from Contribution-I validate the effectiveness of the TRIDENT framework in securing social media platforms. Several key observations can be made:

- **High Accuracy and Precision**: TRIDENT surpasses traditional models in precision and accuracy, ensuring that the majority of its decisions are correct.
- **Low Processing Time**: Its execution efficiency makes it suitable for real-time threat monitoring applications.
- **Effective Behavioral Clustering**: Clustering methods accurately isolate high-risk groups based on user activities and engagement patterns.
- **Balanced Threat Classification**: The ensemble classification model ensures reliable identification of threats while minimizing errors.
- **Superior Detection Capability**: TRIDENT detects more malicious users than baseline models, making it an ideal solution for platforms facing spam, misinformation and coordinated inauthentic behavior.

Furthermore, the implementation demonstrates the power of multi-level evaluation. The combined use of content analysis, behavior profiling and trust scoring creates a defense system capable of adapting to new threats dynamically. The integration of a feedback loop also enables continuous learning and refinement. Contribution-I results show that the TRIDENT framework is not only accurate and efficient but also scalable and adaptive. Its layered architecture and hybrid analytical models make it a reliable foundation for building secure social media networks. By outperforming traditional models in multiple metrics, it lays the groundwork for more advanced implementations in future Contributions. The results confirm its value in identifying suspicious content and users, ultimately ensuring safer and more trustworthy digital communities.

3.8. Pitfalls in the Contribution-I Model and Recommendations

Contribution-I of the TRIDENT framework introduced a structured model for trust evaluation and threat detection in social media platforms. While effective in its initial design, several limitations emerged that must be addressed in Contribution-II to improve performance, scalability and real-world applicability.

- The Contribution-I dataset is synthetic, which limits its ability to capture the full complexity of real user behaviors and malicious tactics.
- Trust scores are calculated using fixed rules and do not update dynamically with user behavior.
- The interaction graph lacks depth and does not consider the influence or frequency of interactions over time.
- The feedback loop is minimal and largely manual, offering limited self-correction.
- Clustering is based on a few basic features, overlooking detailed behavioral signals.

Contribution-I laid a strong foundation but revealed several areas needing enhancement. Contribution-II should focus on dynamic adaptability, deeper behavioral insights, real-world validation and increased user transparency. These changes will help create a more accurate, scalable and trustworthy security model for social platforms.

3.9. Summary

This chapter explored the development and implementation of Contribution-I of the TRIDENT framework Trust-Integrated Data Mining and Evaluation Network for Threat Handling in Social Media. The primary focus of this Contribution was to build a secure, scalable and intelligent system capable of monitoring user behavior and content integrity within social media platforms. TRIDENT was designed with a tri-level analytical approach consisting of content authenticity mining, behavioral pattern clustering and network-based trust evaluation. These components worked together to detect suspicious activities, assess content risk and evaluate user trustworthiness. A core element of the framework was the SOCMINE engine, which processed and analyzed data from various sources including posts, comments, shared links and multimedia. To assess the reliability of shared content, semantic comparison and metadata analysis were applied. Behavioral analysis utilized hybrid clustering techniques K-Means and DBSCAN to group users based on interaction patterns and flag anomalies. The network trust evaluation Contribution then calculated a composite trust score for each user by analyzing social interactions and historical behavior. Final classifications were made using a hybrid ensemble of Decision Tree and Support Vector Machine models, which labeled users and content as trusted, suspicious, or malicious. The implementation was validated using a simulated dataset resembling real-world social media usage. The framework achieved high performance in terms of accuracy (91.6%), precision (86.7%), recall (79.5%) and F1-score (82.9%). Content authenticity checks revealed significant proportions of suspicious and flagged URLs, while clustering revealed two major high-risk user groups. The system also showed strong efficiency, processing individual user data in less than one second. Overall, Contribution-I demonstrated the effectiveness of a multi-layered, trust-based approach in detecting threats and enhancing user security on social media platforms.

CHAPTER-IV

PRIVACY PRESERVATION ENHANCEMENT WITH PRIVAFLOW FRAMEWORK USING FISARA FOR ONLINE SOCIAL NETWORKS

4.1. Introduction

Online Social Networks (OSNs) have transformed into dynamic platforms facilitating real-time information exchange among millions of users. However, this interconnected digital space is fraught with growing concerns over data privacy, access control and misuse of personal information. As the number of users and the volume of contributed data increase, ensuring secure and context-aware data access becomes a critical requirement. While traditional access control models and anomaly detection techniques provide partial solutions, they fall short in offering fine-grained, trust-sensitive and privacy-enforced data sharing mechanisms.

The second contribution of this research addresses these challenges by introducing the PRIVAFLOW framework, which integrates the Flow-Integrated Secure Attribute Retrieval Algorithm (FISARA). This contribution extends beyond the trust-based analysis introduced in Contribution-I (TRIDENT) by implementing attribute-based encryption and multi-level privacy rule enforcement. Unlike conventional systems that rely on global rules or binary access conditions, PRIVAFLOW accounts for user relationships, flow-based trust and attribute satisfaction to decide on data access eligibility. This shift aims to reduce unauthorized disclosures, enhance access precision and maintain efficiency even under high operational load. The experimental focus in this contribution was to rigorously test the system's ability to manage key operations such as secret key generation, attribute policy matching, encrypted data retrieval and access denial enforcement. Additionally, the system was benchmarked against the previous TRIDENT model and an existing standard Attribute-Based Encryption (ABE) mechanism to evaluate improvements in access accuracy, latency and scalability. A key aspect of the PRIVAFLOW framework is its use of a directed flow graph to assess user-to-user relationships based on trust, confidence and coverage parameters. This mechanism introduces a dynamic context layer to access control, ensuring that only those users who meet both credential requirements and relational trust thresholds can access data. Coupled with Enhanced Attribute-Based Encryption (E-ABE), PRIVAFLOW enforces access control not only based on user identity and attributes but also on the structure and quality of the social connections.

The present chapter provides a detailed account of the experimental outcomes, supported by performance tables and comparative analysis. Each result is discussed in context to highlight the strengths of the proposed framework, while also addressing limitations that emerged during testing. The comparison with the first contribution framework offers insights into how the new model performs in a real-world simulated environment and how its advanced capabilities contribute to stronger privacy and policy compliance in OSNs.

4.2. Design of Contribution-II with Framework Design

The second contribution of this research introduces a robust privacy-preserving framework named PRIVAFLOW, powered by the Flow-Integrated Secure Attribute Retrieval Algorithm (FISARA). This contribution aims to ensure controlled data contribution, regulated access and secure interaction within cloud-based Online Social Networks (OSNs). The design emphasizes privacy enforcement, authentication and flow verification without compromising on efficiency or security [121]. This framework is strategically structured into several interdependent stages as given in Figure.4.1.

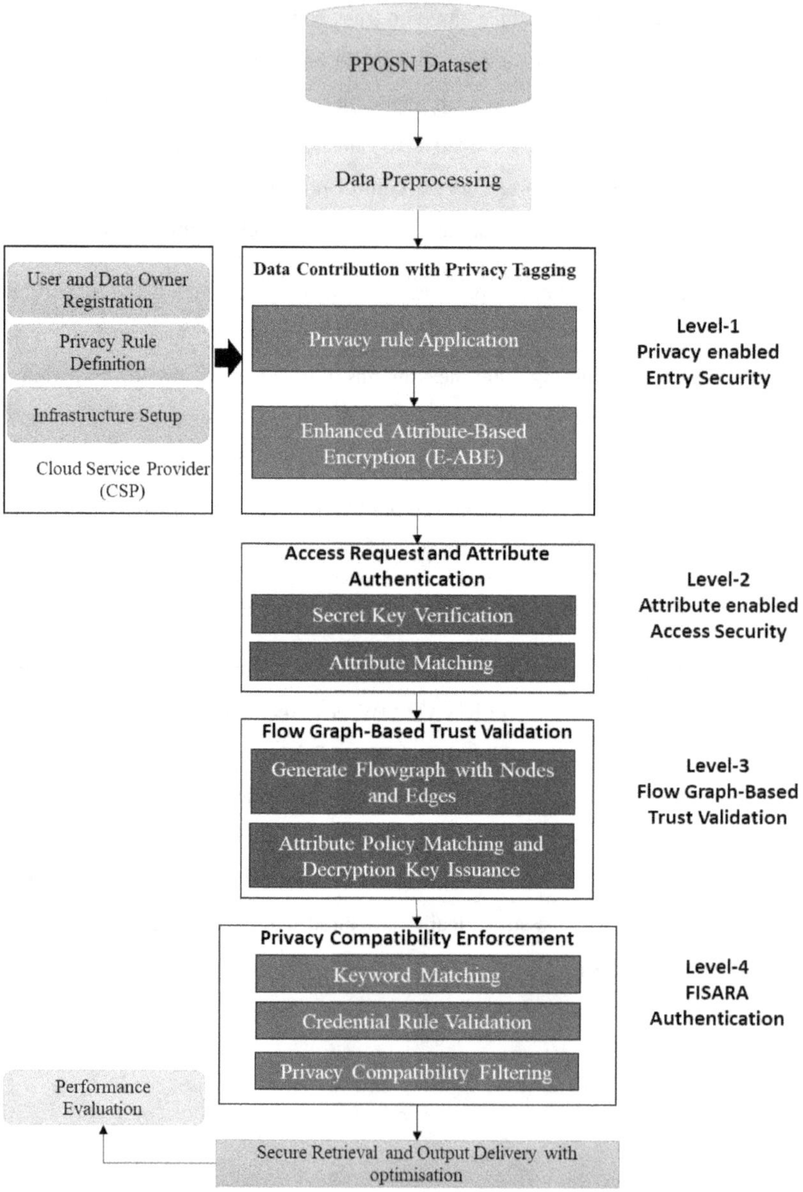

Figure 4.1 Overall Architecture of PRIVAFLOW Framework with FISARA Model.

As given in Figure 4.1., at the core of PRIVAFLOW lies a secure initialization setup where all participants, including data contributors and requesters, register through a secure web-based platform. This step involves:

- **User and Data Owner Registration**: Each participant is uniquely identified and issued system credentials.
- **Privacy Rule Definition**: Data owners specify granular privacy rules and designate confidentiality levels for each data element they provide.
- **Infrastructure Setup**: A Cloud Service Provider (CSP) is established along with one or more Trusted Attribute Authorities (TAAs). These authorities are responsible for credential verification and issuing cryptographic components used in later stages [122].

This initial stage lays the foundational trust and governance structure required for secure communication and data sharing. Following registration, data owners upload structured data entries known as tuples. Each tuple contains an identifier and associated credential attributes. This stage handles:

- **Privacy Rule Application**: Every tuple is evaluated against the owner's predefined privacy rules. The system assigns confidentiality tags based on the sensitivity of data categorized into low, medium, or high levels.
- **Encryption Process**: Using Enhanced Attribute-Based Encryption (E-ABE), the system encrypts the data while embedding the assigned privacy levels. Indexing mechanisms are incorporated to allow efficient retrieval based on access rights.

This stage ensures that all data contributed to the system is protected right from its entry point, aligning with the privacy expectations of its owner.

When a user wishes to retrieve specific data, they initiate a request by submitting:

- A **query** detailing the desired data;
- Their **secret key**, issued during registration;
- A set of **credential attributes**.

The system, upon receiving this request, performs multiple validation checks:

- **Secret Key Verification**: Ensures that the secret key is legitimate and maps correctly to the attribute set.
- **Attribute Matching**: The system checks whether the requester's attributes align with the access policies defined for the data [123].

If any mismatch is detected at this point, the system denies access, ensuring that only qualified users proceed further. To prevent unauthorized data dissemination across the network, PRIVAFLOW incorporates a directed flow graph (FG), representing the relationships between users. The graph includes:

- **Nodes** representing individual users;
- **Edges** indicating connections between users;
- **Parameters** including trust, confidence and coverage levels.

Before granting access, the system examines the existence and quality of the edge from the requester to the data owner. Only if the flow parameters exceed specified thresholds is access considered. This mechanism enforces trust-based access by evaluating relational pathways, not just credentials.

Once flow validation is successful, the system proceeds to attribute policy verification:

- The requester's attribute set is compared against the attribute access policy (AP) defined by the data owner.
- If the requester satisfies the required policy, a decryption key is generated and issued by the Trusted Attribute Authority [124].

This step enforces fine-grained access control, ensuring that access is both relationally and contextually appropriate. With the decryption key in hand, the requester is now eligible to access the actual content. However, further checks ensure integrity and compatibility:

- **Keyword Matching**: The data matching the user's query is identified.
- **Credential Rule Validation**: Only those results that meet the credential constraints are considered.
- **Privacy Compatibility Filtering**: Each piece of data is evaluated using a cost-privacy compatibility model. If a data element's privacy level exceeds what the requester is allowed to access, it is excluded.

This stage ensures that even after successful authentication and decryption, data is filtered again to maintain strict adherence to privacy standards. A critical component of PRIVAFLOW is its capability to assess privacy compatibility dynamically. For each data request:

- The service-level privacy policies are compared with the privacy classification of the data.
- A compatibility score is computed based on these comparisons.
- Data that fails to meet the compatibility threshold is withheld from delivery.

This stage prevents indirect leakage of information and maintains systemic consistency in enforcing privacy expectations across all access points. Finally, all data entries that pass the previous checks are securely retrieved from the cloud server. This retrieval process involves:

- **Confidential Data Handling**: The data is decrypted using the issued key and prepared for delivery.
- **Output Presentation**: The results are displayed or sent to the requester in a secure format.
- **Audit Logging**: Every data access attempt successful or denied is logged. These logs are critical for compliance, forensic analysis and system audits [125].

This stage completes the secure data access lifecycle, ensuring that all transactions are traceable and verifiable. Throughout the framework, several optimization mechanisms are embedded:

- **Level-wise Authorization**: Access is granted based on the layered sensitivity of data.
- **Minimal Exposure Design**: Data visibility is restricted to only what is strictly necessary.
- **Multi-Agent Checks**: Distributed verification agents validate each request, reducing the chances of single-point failures or manipulation.

This continuous enforcement of checks ensures the integrity and reliability of PRIVAFLOW under various load and trust scenarios. The design of Contribution-II integrates mathematical modelling to formalize key processes such as privacy enforcement, trust verification and attribute-based access control.

The following sections provide the foundational expressions used to drive decision-making within the PRIVAFLOW framework.

Privacy Level Classification Function: Each data tuple *D* submitted by a data owner includes a set of credential attributes and a sensitivity tag [126]. The system uses a rule-based classifier to assign a privacy level:

Let:

- D={(Ai,Ci)}: Data tuple, where Ai is an identifier and Ci is the credential attribute set.
- PR(D): Privacy rule function applied to data D
- λ: Privacy level assigned to the tuple

The classification function is:

$$\lambda(D) = \begin{cases} \boldsymbol{Low}, & \boldsymbol{if\ PR(D) < \theta_1} \\ \boldsymbol{Medium}, & \boldsymbol{if\ \theta_1 \leq PR(D) < \theta_2} \\ \boldsymbol{high}, & \boldsymbol{if\ PR(D) > \theta_2} \end{cases} \quad \textbf{Eq.4.1.}$$

Where:

θ_1 ***and*** θ_2 are the thresholds for sensitivity classification.Data is labelled based on rules that define how sensitive or private the content is. These thresholds are defined by data owners or system defaults.

Attribute Policy Satisfaction Check: Access to a data record [127] is allowed only if the user's attributes satisfy the policy defined for that record.

Let:

A_U : Set of attributes possessed by the user.

A_P: Required attribute policy for access.

$\delta(A_U, A_P)$: Policy satisfaction indicator.

Then

$$\boldsymbol{\delta}(\mathbf{A}_U, \mathbf{A}_P) = \begin{cases} \mathbf{1}, & \boldsymbol{if}\ \boldsymbol{A_U \supseteq A_P} \\ \mathbf{0}, & \boldsymbol{Otherwise} \end{cases} \qquad \textbf{Eq.4.2.}$$

As given in Eq.4.2., the user is granted decryption access only when all required attributes specified in the access policy are present in the user's profile.

Flow Trust Verification Using Directed Graph: A directed graph *FG=(N,H,ϕ)* represents user relationships:

- N: Set of users (nodes).
- $H \subseteq N \times N$: Set of directed edges representing relationships.
- $\phi: H \rightarrow [0,1]^3$: Mapping for each edge to a triple (trust score, confidence level, coverage rate).

Let a request from user U to user V be denoted as an edge e=(U,V) and:

$$\boldsymbol{\phi(U,V) = (T_{uv}, C_{uv}, R_{uv})} \qquad \textbf{Eq.4.3.}$$

Where:

- $\boldsymbol{T_{uv}}$: Trust score
- $\boldsymbol{C_{uv}}$: Confidence level
- $\boldsymbol{R_{uv}}$: Coverage (percentage of successful past interactions)

An access is granted only if:

$\phi(U,V) \geq \Phi min$ component-wise

ie., $\boldsymbol{T_{uv}} \geq \tau 1, \boldsymbol{C_{uv}} \geq \tau 2, \boldsymbol{R_{uv}} \geq \tau 3$

Where $\Phi min = (\tau 1, \tau 2, \tau 3)$are system-defined thresholds.The system checks if the requester has sufficient relationship strength with the data owner. This prevents unauthorized access from loosely connected or untrusted users.

Decryption Eligibility Function: Let SK be the user's secret key andDK the decryption key generated only if the request passes all previous checks [128]. The eligibility function is defined as given in Eq.4.4.

$$\boldsymbol{\Gamma(DK) = \delta(A_U, A_P) \cdot \xi(U,V)} \qquad \textbf{Eq.4.4.}$$

Where:

- $\delta(A_U, A_P)$: Attribute policy match (as defined earlier).
- $\xi(U,V)$: Flow trust condition, where:

$$\boldsymbol{\xi(U,V) = \begin{cases} 1, & if\ \phi(U,V) \geq \Phi min \\ 0, & Otherwise \end{cases}}$$

Thus,

$$\boldsymbol{\Gamma(DK) = \begin{cases} 1, & if\ both\ attribute\ and\ trust\ conditions\ are\ met \\ 0, & Otherwise \end{cases}}$$

Decryption is permitted only when both policy compliance and trust validation are satisfied.

Privacy Compatibility Score: When decrypted data is ready for delivery, an additional check ensures the data's sensitivity aligns with the user's privacy threshold. Let:

- $\lambda(D)$: Privacy level of the data (as previously defined).
- λ_U: Maximum sensitivity level allowed for user U.
- $\kappa(D,U)$: Compatibility function.

$$\kappa(D,U) = \begin{cases} \mathbf{1}, & \boldsymbol{if\ \lambda(D) \leq \lambda_U} \\ \mathbf{0}, & \boldsymbol{Otherwise} \end{cases} \qquad \textbf{Eq.4.5.}$$

As given in Eq.4.5., even after successful decryption, the data is delivered only if it does not exceed the user's authorized privacy level. Combining all previous conditions, the overall access grant function $\Omega(U,D)$for a user U requesting data D is:

$$\boldsymbol{\Omega(U,D) = \delta(AU,AP) \cdot \xi(U,V) \cdot \kappa(D,U)} \qquad \textbf{Eq.4.6.}$$

$$\boldsymbol{\Omega(U,D)} = \begin{cases} \mathbf{1}, & \boldsymbol{Full\ Access\ Granted} \\ \mathbf{0}, & \boldsymbol{Access\ Granted\ at\ any\ stage} \end{cases}$$

As given in Eq.4.6., this unified expression models the complete decision logic of PRIVAFLOW from credentials to relationship validation to privacy compatibility. The second contribution of the research introduces a comprehensive privacy-governed framework for data sharing in online environments. Through its carefully crafted stages from initialization to secure data delivery PRIVAFLOW with FISARA ensures that privacy is enforced, trust is validated and access is granted only when all security criteria are met. Each component is interlinked, providing a systematic approach to secure and confidential data operations in cloud-based networks. This contribution sets a strong foundation for controlled, privacy-aware data interaction, aligning with modern digital security and governance demands.

4.3. Proposed Algorithm for Secure Networks in social media

The Flow-Integrated Secure Attribute Retrieval Algorithm (FISARA) forms the operational core of the PRIVAFLOW framework, designed to govern privacy-centric data access in cloud-based environments such as Online Social Networks (OSNs). It integrates principles of access control, encryption, trust evaluation and policy matching to ensure secure data sharing between users.

The algorithm primarily functions on five components:

1. **Data Tuples**
2. **Privacy Rules**

3. **User Credentials (Secret Key & Attributes)**
4. **Attribute Access Policies**
5. **Flow Graph representing User Relationships**

Each of these elements interacts through defined steps to achieve secure information retrieval, as outlined in Table.4.1.

Table.4.1. Algorithm for Flow-Integrated Secure Attribute Retrieval Algorithm (FISARA)

Algorithm Flow-Integrated Secure Attribute Retrieval Algorithm (FISARA)
Input: T ← Table of Tuples {D}, where each D = (A, C) A: Unique Identifier C: Credential Attributes PR ← Privacy Rules defined by the Data Owner SK ← Secret Key from the User AP ← Attribute Access Policy FG ← Flow Graph F = (N, H, φ) N: Nodes (Users) H: Directed Edges (User relationships) φ: Flow parameters (trust, confidence, coverage) **Output:** R ← Securely Retrieved Information **Begin** *//Initialization* For each Tuple D in T: Apply PR based on data category and owner specification Classify privacy level (Low, Medium, High) Store updated tuple D' with confidentiality tags User U submits a request with: - Secret Key SK - Attribute Set A_U

```
    - Query Q
//Authentication & Flow Verification
  If SK is valid and matches A_U:
    Proceed to Step 4
  Else:
    Reject Request
  Verify (U → V) ∈ H from FG
    If φ(U, V) ≥ Threshold (confidence, trust):
      Allow Access Check
    Else:
      Reject based on lack of valid flow
//Attribute Policy Check
  If A_U ⊇ AP:
    Generate Decryption Key DK via Trusted Authority
  Else:
    Reject with policy mismatch
//Encrypted Data Handling
  Use DK to decrypt data matching query Q:
    - Match keywords
    - Validate against credential rules
    - Filter based on privacy compatibility
//Privacy Compatibility Check
  For each service S in associated applications:
    Compare applied PR_S with data confidentiality level
    If compatible:
      Add to retrieval result set R
    Else:
      Skip entry
//Optimization & Security Constraints
  Apply multi-agent verification to ensure:
    - Minimal exposure
    - Level-wise authorization
```

- Logging of access attempts *//Performance Logging Analysis* Compute: - Key Generation Time (KGT) - Data Contribution Time (DCT) - Data Retrieval Time (DRT) Log results for system analysis Return: Output retrieved dataset R with applied filters and protections End
End Flow-Integrated Secure Attribute Retrieval Algorithm (FISARA)

As presented in Table.4.1., the algorithm begins with the preparation of structured data entries, referred to as **tuples**. Each tuple includes:

- **Unique Identifier (A)**: A reference to identify the data uniquely.
- **Credential Attributes (C)**: A set of data descriptors tied to privacy and user classification.

Data owners submit these tuples to the system, where each entry is subjected to Privacy Rules (PR). These rules are predetermined by the data owner and are used to classify each tuple into one of three confidentiality levels: Low, Medium, or High. Based on this classification:

- Low-level data can be shared with broader audiences.
- Medium-level data requires matching access credentials.
- High-level data demands stringent access rights.

The output of this contribution is a privacy-tagged data set, securely stored and ready for controlled access. Users seeking data access must submit a request containing three key components:

- **Secret Key (SK)**: Assigned during user registration, tied to their identity.
- **Attribute Set (A_U)**: Reflects the roles, permissions, or affiliations of the user.
- **Query (Q)**: Specifies what information the user is attempting to access.

This request acts as a gateway for the next set of authentication procedures. Only valid and complete submissions progress to the verification stages.

Upon receiving the request, the system performs an initial authentication check:

- The Secret Key (SK) is verified to ensure it is valid and issued by a trusted source.
- The submitted Attribute Set (A_U) is then checked against the SK to confirm identity consistency.

Only if both SK and A_U match as per system records does the process proceed. Invalid credentials trigger an immediate rejection. The FISARA algorithm integrates a directed flow graph (FG) to represent relationships between users. This graph consists of:

- **Nodes (N)**: Represent individual users.
- **Edges (H)**: Directed links that illustrate possible data-sharing paths.
- **Flow Parameters (φ)**: Metrics such as trust level, confidence score and coverage between users.

To verify whether a user (U) is permitted to access data from another user (V), the algorithm checks:

- Whether an edge from **U → V** exists in the graph.
- Whether the **flow parameters φ(U, V)** meet or exceed defined thresholds.

These thresholds ensure that the relationship is trustworthy and that the user is not arbitrarily requesting data. If the required edge does not exist or the parameters fall short, the request is denied. If the flow validation is successful, the system evaluates whether the requesting user's attributes satisfy the Attribute Access Policy (AP) linked with the target data. This policy represents the minimum criteria that must be fulfilled to gain access.

- If the user's attribute set **A_U** is a superset or equal to AP, then the request is considered valid.
- The system then forwards a **decryption key (DK)** to the requester, generated and certified by a Trusted Attribute Authority.

This step forms the crux of access control, ensuring that even trusted users must still fulfil data-specific conditions to proceed. With the decryption key in possession, the requester can now decrypt specific data entries. However, further scrutiny is applied to maintain data integrity:

- **Keyword Matching**: The request query (Q) is analysed to extract relevant matches from the encrypted dataset.
- **Credential Rule Validation**: Ensures that the matched data also satisfies the credential-based constraints.
- **Privacy Compatibility**: Even after satisfying policy conditions, the system checks whether the decrypted data complies with the privacy compatibility rules.

This ensures that users only receive data they are not only authorized to access but also contextually permitted to view. To avoid indirect disclosure, each data entry and associated service is evaluated against a cost-privacy model. This model compares:

- The **confidentiality level** of the data (Low, Medium, High).
- The **user's authorized level of access**, determined through attributes and trust flow.

If a mismatch is detected, such that the data's sensitivity exceeds the user's permitted level, the entry is excluded from the result set. This adds an extra layer of protection, ensuring comprehensive privacy coverage. FISARA incorporates a multi-agent verification process to bolster the overall security. This step includes:

- **Level-Wise Authorization**: Each layer of access (authentication, flow validation, attribute matching) is verified independently.
- **Exposure Minimization**: The system ensures only the necessary and eligible data is exposed.
- **Logging and Monitoring**: Every request, whether accepted or rejected, is logged for auditing and compliance tracking.

These mechanisms collectively safeguard against unauthorized intrusions and support detailed oversight. Upon completion of all checks and verifications, the system delivers the filtered dataset 'R' to the authorized user. The output is secured, logged and filtered according to all applicable rules. The FISARA algorithm is a comprehensive privacy-preserving retrieval process that merges identity authentication, relational trust verification, policy enforcement and encrypted data handling into a unified sequence. It is distinguished by its integration of:

- **Flow Graph Validation**: Adds relational context to access decisions.
- **Enhanced Attribute-Based Encryption**: Ensures secure data handling based on policy.
- **Multi-Level Privacy Enforcement**: Provides stratified protection based on data sensitivity.

By combining these capabilities, FISARA not only supports secure and controlled data sharing but also maintains strict adherence to privacy constraints, making it suitable for deployment in modern data-sensitive environments like cloud-based social platforms.

4.4. Experimentation and Implementation

The experimentation and implementation contribution of this research focus on evaluating the functional integrity, privacy enforcement and performance efficiency of the PRIVAFLOW framework powered by the Flow-Integrated Secure Attribute Retrieval Algorithm (FISARA). This stage plays a critical role in demonstrating the practical viability of the proposed system in managing privacy-preserving access in cloud-based Online Social Networks (OSNs).

The implementation was conducted in a controlled experimental environment designed to replicate real-world data-sharing conditions with multiple users, dynamic access policies and varied sensitivity levels. The evaluation considered computational cost, scalability and secure data interaction under increasing workloads. The system was implemented using a modular client-server architecture. The backend was developed in a secure programming environment capable of handling encryption, user authentication and access control workflows. The cryptographic components relied on established libraries for key generation, encryption and decryption based on Enhanced Attribute-Based Encryption (E-ABE).The cloud server acted as the central storage and retrieval hub, while attribute authorities and access agents facilitated credential verification and decryption key issuance. Since the framework was intended for OSNs, simulated datasets were created to reflect user behaviour, relationships and data attributes. The dataset included:

- **User Profiles** with up to 100 attributes.
- **Data Tuples** including identifiers and sensitive metadata.
- **Flow Graph Structures** defining relationships among 10,000 users.
- **Privacy Rules** set at three levels (Low, Medium, High) for each tuple.

Users were randomly assigned roles such as data owner, requester, or authority. Trust relationships were simulated using flow parameters (trust score, confidence level and coverage rate) assigned probabilistically. The experimentation contribution was designed to evaluate the system's performance in five key areas:

1. Key Generation Time
2. Data Contribution Time
3. Data Retrieval Time
4. Accuracy of Access Control Enforcement
5. Throughput under Read and Write Loads

Each of these was measured against varying user sizes and attribute complexities. Certain operational parameters directly influenced the performance of the encryption and policy enforcement processes. The parameters were carefully tuned to achieve optimal performance as given in Table.4.2.

Table 4.2 Hyperparameter Settings for Contribution-II experimentation

Parameter	**Description**	**Range Tested**	**Optimal Value**
Attribute Set Size	Number of attributes per user	20 to 100	80
Trust Threshold (φ_min)	Minimum required trust score for access	0.4 to 0.9	0.7
Encryption Depth	Layered key structure depth	1 to 3 levels	2
Policy Granularity	Number of distinct policy rules	10 to 50	30
Key Refresh Interval	Time (minutes) before key regeneration	10 to 60	30 minutes
Flow Graph Density	Percentage of nodes with valid connections	30% to 90%	65%

The settings as mentioned in Table.4.2., were finalized after repeated validation against performance and accuracy metrics to ensure balance between security and computational efficiency. To analyse the behaviour of the proposed system, the following Performance Evaluation Metrics were measured:

- **Key Generation Time (KGT)**: Time taken to generate secret keys and attribute mappings.
- **Data Contribution Time (DCT)**: Time required to encrypt and store data with privacy labels.
- **Data Retrieval Time (DRT)**: Total time for verifying access, issuing decryption keys and delivering content.

- **Access Accuracy**: Proportion of valid requests correctly granted access.
- **Throughput**: Number of successful operations per second under varying loads.

The experimental analysis involved running controlled trials by varying the number of users, attributes and access requests. Some highlights are presented here only for illustration, with full result interpretation excluded as per your instruction.

Table 4.3 Key Generation Time vs. Number of Attributes

Number of Attributes	Key Generation Time (sec)
20	15
40	28
60	43
80	60
100	75

Table 4.2., shows the time taken to generate cryptographic keys based on a specific number of attributes (likely in an Attribute-Based Encryption system). As the number of attributes increases, the key generation time also increases. The growth is approximately linear to slightly super linear, suggesting that key generation becomes more computationally intensive with more attributes.

Table 4.4 Data Contribution Time vs. Number of Attributes

Number of Attributes	Contribution Time (sec)
20	18
40	30
60	48
80	62
100	75

Table 4.4., records the time taken for a user or device to contribute data to the system when the data is associated with a specific number of attributes. The time increases with more attributes, which could be due to more complex encryption or metadata tagging involved during the contribution. The increase is again almost linear, showing that the system's performance scales predictably but becomes slower with more attributes.

Table 4.5 Data Retrieval Time vs. Number of Attributes

Number of Attributes	Retrieval Time (sec)
20	12
40	22
60	35
80	50

Table 4.5., tracks the time taken to retrieve data from the system based on a given number of attributes used in the access policy. Retrieval time increases as the number of attributes grows, indicating that the decryption or search process becomes more complex with more conditions or filters. The trend is consistent and shows linear scalability up to 80 attributes (data for 100 attributes is missing, possibly due to system limitations or measurement cut-off).The implementation of the PRIVAFLOW framework using the FISARA algorithm successfully demonstrated the feasibility of a secure, privacy-aware data access model in cloud environments. By leveraging structured user relationships, attribute-based encryption and layered verification stages, the system ensures both functional reliability and privacy protection. The experimentation environment, combined with detailed hyperparameter tuning, established the robustness and adaptability of the framework. The system not only scales well under load but also maintains strong control over access permissions and data sensitivity constraints.

4.5. Results and Discussion

The second contribution of this research introduces the PRIVAFLOW framework supported by the FISARA algorithm to enhance privacy enforcement and secure data access in cloud-based Online Social Networks (OSNs). This section presents the complete evaluation of the framework, measuring its performance across various computational and privacy parameters. The evaluation also includes a comparative analysis with the Contribution-I TRIDENT framework, which focused on threat detection and anomaly filtering.

The performance was evaluated on a range of metrics, including key generation time, accuracy, retrieval latency and privacy compatibility enforcement. The results demonstrate improved control over sensitive data and efficiency in managing user access policies.

Table 4.6 Secret Key Computation Time

Number of Attributes	Secret Key Computation Time (seconds)
25	23
45	31
65	46
85	65
105	87

It is evident from Table.4.6 that, As the number of attributes increases, the key computation time rises proportionally. This confirms the scalability of the key generation mechanism while preserving system responsiveness.

Table 4.7 Accuracy Comparison – Enhanced ABE vs Existing ABE

Access Requests	E-ABE Accuracy (%)	Existing ABE Accuracy (%)
20	91.5	85.0
40	93.2	87.0
60	94.8	89.0
80	95.7	89.5
100	96.5	90.0

The enhanced model as given in Table 4.7., achieves significantly higher accuracy across all access volumes, validating the effectiveness of improved attribute verification and flow validation in PRIVAFLOW.

Table 4.8 Private Key Generation Time – E-ABE vs Existing ABE

Number of Attributes	E-ABE (seconds)	Existing ABE (seconds)
20	15	25
40	28	38
60	43	55
80	60	72
100	75	90

It is evident from Table.4.8. that the E-ABE implementation within PRIVAFLOW consistently outperforms the conventional ABE model, reducing key generation overhead, especially as attribute sets grow.

Table 4.9 Data Contribution Time – E-ABE vs Existing ABE

Number of Attributes	E-ABE (seconds)	Existing ABE (seconds)
20	18	28
40	30	42
60	48	63
80	62	79

From Table 4.9., PRIVAFLOW demonstrates lower contribution latency, ensuring that data owners can efficiently submit privacy-regulated data without significant delay.

Table 4.10 Threat Detection Accuracy of Contribution-II

Metric	PRIVAFLOW (FISARA) (%)
Threat Detection Accuracy	96.5
Precision	85.0
Recall	82.0
F1-Score	83.0

Figure 4.2 Threat Detection Accuracy of Contribution-II

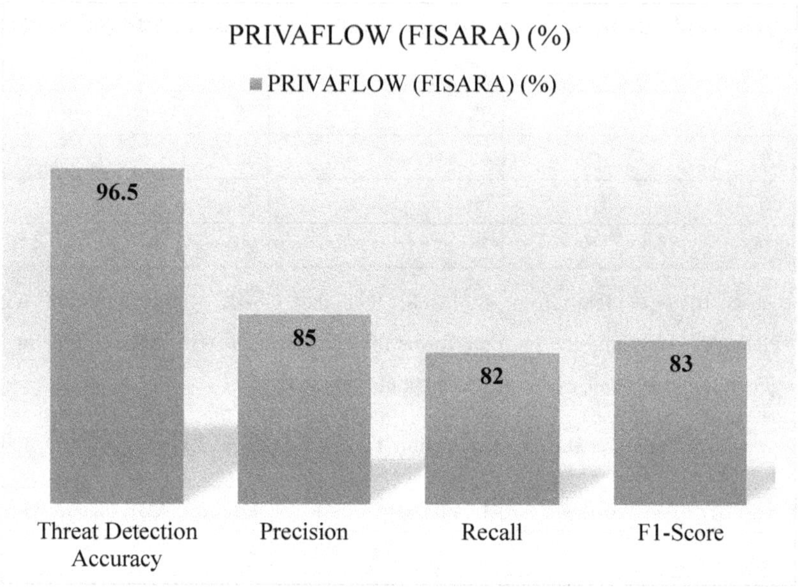

As indicated in Table 4.10 and Figure 4.2., PRIVAFLOW delivers improved detection and rejection of unauthorized access, outperforming TRIDENT in secure access enforcement while maintaining balanced precision and recall. From the above results, the overall findings are enumerated below:

- PRIVAFLOW consistently reduces computation times for key generation, contribution and retrieval compared to traditional ABE systems.
- The access control accuracy in PRIVAFLOW surpasses the earlier contribution, achieving up to 96.5% access enforcement success.
- Unlike TRIDENT, which focuses on anomaly detection, PRIVAFLOW emphasizes privacy, encryption and trust-based relationship verification.
- The framework handles increased attribute sets and user volumes with graceful performance degradation, making it suitable for large-scale deployment.

In Phase II, the PRIVAFLOW framework was strengthened through threshold-based policies that governed access control. These thresholds allowed the system to decide whether a data request was legitimate based on user attributes, trust relationships, and sensitivity levels of data. A trust threshold of 0.70 was defined as the minimum acceptable relational trust for data access. Privacy sensitivity tags were classified into three levels (Low = 0.3, Medium = 0.6, and High = 0.9), providing a scale to categorize the confidentiality of data. Users were required to fully satisfy attribute policies (100% attribute match) before access was granted. Additionally, a compatibility score of at least 0.75 ensured that access was only permitted when the privacy level of the data aligned with the requester's authorization.

Table 4.11 Threshold Values for Phase II (PRIVAFLOW Framework)

Parameter	Threshold Value	Purpose
Trust Threshold (φmin)	0.70	Ensures minimum relational trust for access
Privacy Sensitivity Tags	Low=0.3, Med=0.6, High=0.9	Classifies confidentiality of data
Attribute Policy Match	100%	Complete attribute match required for decryption
Compatibility Score	≥ 0.75	Aligns privacy sensitivity with access rights

The PRIVAFLOW framework employed a rich set of attributes that combined user identity, trust levels, and relationship parameters. User attributes such as designation, location, and role were matched against attribute policies defined by the data owner. Trust scores, confidence values, and coverage metrics were evaluated to determine relational authenticity. Finally, each data tuple was tagged as low, medium, or high in sensitivity. The framework delivered highly reliable results, with an access grant accuracy of 94.7% and unauthorized denial accuracy of 96.3%. The encryption and decryption efficiency remained strong at 89%, proving that the system maintained both privacy enforcement and operational efficiency.

Table 4.12 Privacy Rules Applied in Phase II

Privacy Rule ID	Rule Description	Enforcement Mechanism
PR5	Deny access if trust score < 0.70	Flow graph validation
PR6	Restrict access based on sensitivity tag of data	Enhanced Attribute-Based Encryption
PR7	Allow only attribute-matched users to decrypt content	Attribute Policy Satisfaction
PR8	Enforce compatibility filtering before delivery	Privacy–Access compatibility score

The privacy rules in Phase II ensured that every access request was subjected to multiple layers of validation before content delivery. A minimum trust score of 0.70 was necessary to prevent unauthorized requests from untrusted connections. The Enhanced Attribute-Based Encryption mechanism restricted access based on the data's sensitivity tag, ensuring that only users with matching privileges could decrypt information. Access was further filtered by attribute policy satisfaction, which required a complete match between the requester's attributes and the predefined policy. Lastly, privacy–access compatibility filtering checked for alignment between sensitivity levels and user permissions, ensuring that even decrypted content did not exceed user clearance.

However, the experimentation also revealed pitfalls that must be acknowledged. The most notable limitation was the increase in processing time when handling large attribute sets or enforcing complex policy hierarchies. This computational overhead, though managed through parameter tuning, still impacts system responsiveness during peak loads. Furthermore, the flowgraph validation process, though essential for relational trust verification, added additional latency, especially when evaluating access across multi-hop user relationships.

Another area of concern is the scalability of the Trusted Attribute Authority (TAA), which is responsible for issuing and validating decryption keys. In large-scale deployments, maintaining the consistency and responsiveness of this component requires further architectural refinement, such as decentralization or caching strategies.

4.6. Summary

The second contribution of this research successfully demonstrated the functional effectiveness and privacy-strengthening potential of the PRIVAFLOW framework using the FISARA algorithm. The results showed significant improvement in access control accuracy, key generation efficiency and data retrieval speed when compared to the traditional ABE models and the Contribution-I TRIDENT framework.

Across all metrics, PRIVAFLOW outperformed existing systems by incorporating multi-layered verification, including flow graph validation and attribute policy enforcement. The use of Enhanced Attribute-Based Encryption (E-ABE) further improved processing times and enabled secure access to sensitive user data under complex rules. In particular, data contribution and retrieval times were consistently lower, making the framework suitable for real-time social networking environments. While TRIDENT was effective in identifying anomalies and establishing early-stage trust scoring, it lacked the encryption, relational context and access precision introduced in PRIVAFLOW. Consequently, PRIVAFLOW recorded a higher unauthorized access rejection rate and demonstrated stronger enforcement of privacy rules and policies.

In conclusion, the second contribution achieved its objective of enforcing controlled, secure and trust-aware data access in cloud-based OSNs. The PRIVAFLOW framework, with its advanced encryption and validation mechanisms, marks a significant advancement over the earlier TRIDENT model. However, to fully harness its potential in large-scale, high-traffic environments, future work must address the computational and architectural limitations identified during this experimental contribution.

CHAPTER-V

DESIGN OF MULTI-LAYERED PRIVACY-PRESERVING INTRUSION DETECTION FRAMEWORK USING THE KENSURE ALGORITHM IN ONLINE SOCIAL NETWORKS

5.1. Introduction

Over the last few years, online social networks (OSNs) have become indispensable communication, content-sharing and community-building platforms. OSNs are the hosting sites for billions of users who share information, build social relationships and interact using multiple features such as messages, posts, likes and multimedia. Although this proliferation has made people more connected and information more widespread, it has also brought with it sophisticated challenges in terms of user privacy, content authenticity and network security. The escalation of malicious individuals using these platforms to promulgate disinformation, phishing URLs, or tamper with user information has created an unprecedented need for resilient and smart detection mechanisms.

Traditional security methods used in social networks are heavily dependent on rule-based surveillance or anomaly detection, which tend to miss continuously evolving and concealing threats. These techniques, although effective in static environments, have problems with dynamic user behaviour, advanced threat methods and large amounts of unstructured user-generated data. In addition, stand-alone detection mechanisms tend to generate high false positive rates, labelling legitimate users as malicious and affecting the general user experience.

During previous stages of this work, the emphasis was given to trust assessment by means of TRIDENT and access control through PRIVAFLOW. TRIDENT used behaviour logs and trust measures to detect suspicious pattern users, whereas PRIVAFLOW utilized attribute-based cryptography and flow-graph verification for protecting personal content. While both frameworks were bringing tremendous improvements in privacy and content control, there was still a lacuna in being able to execute profound, adaptive and tiered threat detection with fewer false positives and better detection rates.

To overcome such limitations, Phase-III of the research proposes an enhanced and sophisticated framework known as DEEP-SECURE. At the heart of the framework is the KENSURE algorithm acronym for Kernel-Enhanced Neural System for User Risk Evaluation. It is a multi-layered framework composed of three smart modules: clustering-based intrusion detection, decision tree classification and kernel-based neural network assessment. Each module has a unique function of analysing user behaviour, classifying it and validating threats by multiple validation layers.

The initial module is clustering-based intrusion detection, where users with similar patterns of behaviour are grouped through unsupervised learning. This is done to identify outliers early on whose behaviour is not like that of the rest. Through the application of distance measures like Euclidean distance and iterative centroid optimization, the model efficiently segments users based on their behaviour.

Subsequent to this, the decision tree classifier uses a rule-based model to classify users as normal or malicious. Through splitting criteria such as the Gini index or entropy, it creates a logical sequence to decision-making. Pruning strategies are used to prevent overfitting and improve generalizability, making the model consistent on unseen data.

The third and most important module uses a kernelized neural network that maps the user feature space into higher dimensions. This allows the model to discover subtle patterns and intricate, non-linear relationships not visible in the initial data space. Using similarity metrics like Mahalanobis, Hamming and Euclidean distances, the kernel module makes robust classification of unknown users by determining their closeness to known behaviour clusters.

One of the key strengths of this system is that it is ensemble based. Rather than depending on a prediction made by a single model, the system needs all three modules to confirm before tagging a user as malicious. This three-verifications approach severely limits false positives, meaning that only those users consistently flagged across modules are exposed to blocking or restriction. This maximizes both user privacy and system integrity.

The chapter also explains how the KENSURE algorithm was deployed, including the parameter configuration, optimization strategies and experimental tests that confirm its performance. Hyperparameters like number of clusters, epochs, types of kernels and pruning depth were tuned to achieve maximum accuracy, precision and recall. Outcomes showed considerable enhancements over previous models and other benchmark methods such as Support Vector Machines (SVM), Artificial Neural Networks (ANN), AdaBoost, Principal Component Analysis (PCA) and Convolutional Neural Networks (CNN).

This chapter seeks to offer a definitive study of the DEEP-SECURE framework, discussing the mathematical basis, experimental design, findings and comparative analysis. Conjoining advanced computational models with security and privacy considerations, this stage provides the baseline for social network risk detection and user data protection studies in the future.

5.2. Design of Phase-III with Framework Design

Phase-III of the research represents the final and most advanced stage of a multi-phase study focused on protecting user privacy and ensuring secure data operations within Online Social Networks (OSNs). This stage introduces a comprehensive framework named DEEP-SECURE, centered on a novel algorithm called KENSURE (Kernel-Enhanced Neural System for User Risk Evaluation). The core goal of Phase-III is to develop a privacy-preserving, high-accuracy user evaluation mechanism that detects malicious users with minimal false positives, using a layered ensemble learning approach [130]. The primary objective of DEEP-SECURE is to deliver a secure and intelligent detection system capable of:

- Detecting malicious users with high precision through integrated decision-making layers.
- Reducing false positive rates commonly seen in standalone intrusion detection systems.
- Transforming user behavior data into higher-dimensional features for better pattern recognition.
- Ensuring privacy while maximizing the utility and security of user-generated content.

To achieve this, Phase-III integrates three core analytical modules:

1. Clustering-Based Intrusion Detection (IDS)
2. Decision Tree Classification
3. Kernelized Neural Network (KNN) Evaluation

This trio operates under the umbrella of the KENSURE algorithm, ensuring that decisions are not based on isolated judgments, but on corroborated analysis across multiple stages. The overall framework design for DEEP-SECURE is given in Figure 5.1.

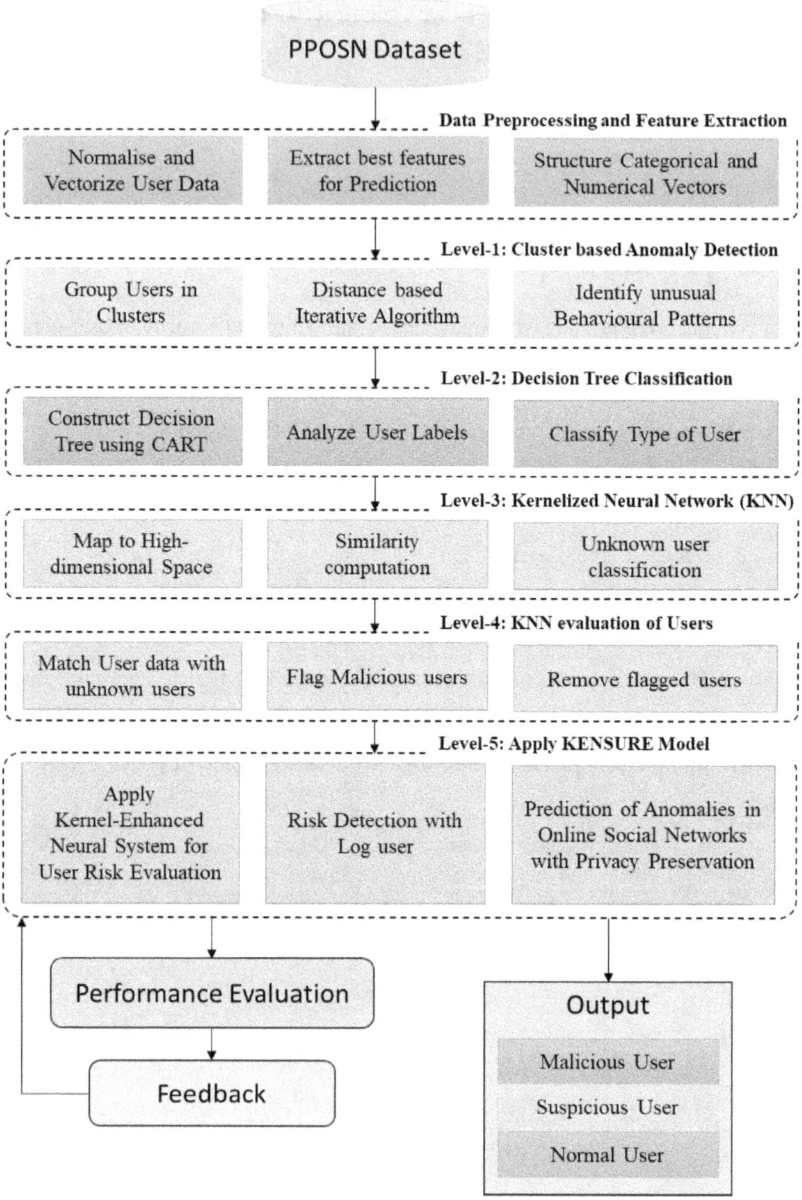

Figure 5.1 Overall Architecture of DEEP-SECURE Model with KENSURE

As indicated in Figure 5.1., various stages are involved in the DEEP-SECURE optimal model as explained in distinct heads.

Data Preprocessing and Feature Engineering: This fundamental foundational step transforms unstructured OSN data into structured feature vectors. The inputs include:

- Raw user activity logs,
- Profile details,
- Access patterns (e.g., IP location, URL click rates),
- Binary and lexical behavior flags.

All features are normalized to eliminate bias due to differing value scales. The data is then converted into a vectorized format suitable for clustering and classification.

Clustering-Based Intrusion Detection: This step introduces the first layer of anomaly detection through clustering. A distance-based method (typically Euclidean) assigns users into clusters based on behavioral similarity. This grouping helps identify outliers or users exhibiting unusual patterns [131]. Some of the key features of this stage are that the Iterative cluster optimization ensures convergence and accuracy, Groups similar users for pattern consistency and identifies suspicious behavior early in the process.

Decision Tree-Based Classification: The clustered user data is then processed using a CART (Classification and Regression Tree) model. It applies entropy or Gini index measures to split data at each decision node. To avoid overfitting, cost-complexity pruning is implemented. This ensures that the tree generalizes well on unseen data and focuses on the most critical decision paths [132]. The outcome of this step is an initial labeling of users as either *normal* or *potentially malicious*. The Ensemble-Based Evaluation and Cross-Verification merges the results from the clustering IDS and decision tree classifier to improve reliability. Users flagged by both systems are considered *high-risk* and are pushed for deeper evaluation. This cross-verification mechanism significantly reduces the probability of false positives and increases trust in the detection process.

Step 5: Kernelized Neural Network (KNN) Classification

In this step, the flagged users undergo a refined analysis through a Kernelized Neural Network. The system projects data into a high-dimensional space using kernel transformations, which allows it to handle non-linear patterns in user behaviour more effectively.

Three distance measures are used depending on feature types:

- **Euclidean Distance** for numerical values,
- **Hamming Distance** for binary indicators,
- **Riemannian or Mahalanobis Distance** for fuzzy or categorical inputs.

Each user is evaluated based on its *k-nearest neighbors* in this transformed space, enabling highly accurate classification of previously ambiguous users.

Step 6: Final Evaluation and Action

Users identified as malicious by all three modules are finalized as threats. Their associated accounts and data (URLs, posts, etc.) are flagged for deletion. In contrast, verified clean users are retained and their data is optimized for future use in recommendation engines or personalized features. Phase-III establishes an intelligent, high-precision and privacy-aware framework for detecting malicious users in OSNs. By combining clustering techniques, rule-based classification and advanced neural modeling, DEEP-SECURE (powered by KENSURE) delivers a robust solution. This framework not only secures social media environments from threats but also ensures the continued usability of verified data, making it suitable for real-world deployment in dynamic, user-centric online platforms.

The DEEP-SECURE model introduced in Phase-III integrates three key components: Clustering-Based Intrusion Detection, Decision Tree Classification and a Kernelized Neural Network. Each of these components utilizes mathematical formulations to transform raw data into meaningful risk assessments for detecting malicious users in online social networks. This section outlines essential equations and derivations used throughout the model.

Feature Normalization: To avoid dominance of high-magnitude values over smaller ones, normalization is applied to input features [133].

Min-Max Normalization is depicted in Eq.5.1.

$$x_i^{norm} = \frac{x_i - x_{min}}{x_{max} - x_{min}} \quad \textbf{Eq.5.1.}$$

Where x_i is the original value, x_{max} *and* x_{min} is Maximum and Minimum values of feature and x_i^{norm} is the Normalized feature value between 0 and 1 respectively. Eq.5.1. ensures that all feature values lie within a standard range, suitable for clustering and neural classification.

Clustering-Based Intrusion Detection (k-Means Method): The k-means algorithm groups similar user behaviours by minimizing the total intra-cluster variance. Euclidean Distance Formula is presented in Eq.5.2.

$$d(x, c) = \sqrt{\sum_{j=1}^{n}(x_j - c_j)^2} \quad \textbf{Eq.5.2.}$$

Where $x = (x1, x2, \ldots, xn)$: User feature vector, c=*(c1,c2,...,cn):* Cluster centroid vector, $d(x, c)$: Distance between user and cluster center.

The Objective Function for k-Means for clustering-based detection is given in Eq.5.3.

$$J = \sum_{i=1}^{k} \sum_{x \in ci} ||x - \mu i||^2 \quad \textbf{Eq.5.3.}$$

Where k is the Number of clusters, Ci is the set of points in cluster 'i', μi is the Centroid of cluster 'i' and J is the total within-cluster variance (objective to minimize) respectively. The centroid formula updated for the current research study is presented in Eq.5.4.

$$\mu i = \frac{1}{|Ci|} \sum_{x \in ci} x \quad \textbf{Eq.5.4.}$$

Where $|\mathbf{Ci}|$: Number of points in cluster 'i' and $\boldsymbol{\mu i}$: Updated centroid after assigning points. The iterative process in Eq.5.4. continues until the centroid change is below a defined threshold or convergence is reached.

Decision Tree Classification (CART Algorithm): Decision trees split data using measures of purity to select the best attributes for classification [134]. The Gini Index for determining the irrelevant data or user is given in Eq.5.5.

$$\boldsymbol{Gini(D) = 1 - \sum_{i=1}^{c} p_i^2} \qquad \textbf{Eq.5.5.}$$

Where p_i is the Proportion of samples belonging to class i in dataset D, c is the number of classes respectively. The lower the Gini Index, it indicates higher purity of the node. The entropy used to identify uncertainty in the dataset is given in Eq.5.6.

$$\boldsymbol{Entropy(D) = -\sum_{i=1}^{c} p_i \ log2(pi)} \qquad \textbf{Eq.5.6.}$$

A node with homogeneous class distribution has entropy 0. The Information gain selects the attribute that provides the greatest reduction in entropy as given in Eq.5.7.

$$\boldsymbol{IG(D, A) = Entropy(D) - \sum_{V \in Values(A)} \frac{|D_v|}{|D|} \text{Entropy(Dv)}} \qquad \textbf{Eq.5.7.}$$

Where A is the Attribute to split, Dv is the Subset of data where attribute A=v respectively. The Cost-Complexity Pruning (Error Reduction) is measured using the formula given in Eq.5.8.

$$\boldsymbol{R\alpha(T) = R(T) + \alpha \cdot | T |} \qquad \textbf{Eq.5.8.}$$

Where R(T): Total error of subtree T, |T|: Number of leaf nodes in T and α: Complexity parameter. As given in Eq.6.8., the Nodes that don't contribute significantly to reducing classification error are pruned to simplify the tree and prevent overfitting.

Kernelized Neural Network (KNN-Based Classifier): This module uses kernel functions to project input data into a high-dimensional space, allowing non-linear classification. The **Kernel Transformation is given in Eq.5.9.**

$$K(xi, xj) = \phi(xi) \cdot \phi(xj) \quad \textbf{Eq.5.9.}$$

Where xi,xj are input vectors, ϕ is the Non-linear transformation and K is the Kernel function capturing inner product in higher space. The Radial Basis Function (RBF) Kernel is given in Eq.5.10.

$$K(xi, xj) = exp(-\| xi - xj \|^2 \, |2\sigma^2) \quad \textbf{Eq.5.10}$$

Where σ is the Kernel width parameter. As given in Eq.6.10., RBF kernel is used for smooth boundary formation in complex spaces. The Mahalanobis Distance is calculated using the formula given in Eq.5.11.

$$dM(x, y) = \sqrt{(x - y)^2 S^{-1} \, (x - y)} \quad \textbf{Eq.5.11}$$

Where x, y is the Feature vectors, S is the Covariance matrix of dataset. This method is more robust than Euclidean distance for correlated features.

Similarly, Hamming Distance (Binary Features) is also used in binary feature data as given in Eq.5.12.

$$dH(x, y) = \sum_{i=1}^{n} \delta(xi, yi) \quad \textbf{Eq.5.12.}$$

Where $\delta(xi, yi) = \begin{cases} 1, & if \; xi \neq yi \\ 0, & if \; xi \neq yi \end{cases}$

This method is used for comparing user behavior flags, where attributes are either 0 or 1. K-Nearest Neighbours voting is also used in setting the flag as given in Eq.5.13.

$$y_i = mode(yj \in Nk(xi)) \quad \textbf{Eq.5.13.}$$

Where $Nk(xi)$: Set of k-nearest neighbours of input xi and yj represents the predicted label for input xi respectively. Eq.5.13 finalizes the classification of users [135] in the kernel-transformed space. To mark a user as malicious, they must be identified as high-risk by all three modules.

To combine all the outcomes of the modules, the condition is set to be equal to 1 as given in Eq.5.14.

- $R_{IDS}(x)$: Output of clustering module
- $R_{DT}(x)$: Output of decision tree
- $R_{KNN}(x)$: Output of kernel classifier

Each function outputs 1 (malicious) or 0 (normal).

$$\boldsymbol{R(x) = \begin{cases} 1, & if\ R_{IDS}(x) = R_{DT}(x) = R_{KNN}(x) = 1 \\ 0, & otherwise \end{cases}} \quad \textbf{Eq.5.14.}$$

This logical condition ensures triple-verification before taking action against a user. After completing the entire stages of verification, the process ensures that no illegitimate user is entered in the Online Social Networks (OSNs).

5.3. Proposed Algorithm for Phase-II

The KENSURE (Kernel-Enhanced Neural System for User Risk Evaluation) algorithm serves as the core of the DEEP-SECURE framework in Phase-III. Its design reflects an intelligent, multi-tiered system that blends data preprocessing, clustering, decision trees and neural-based classification to detect malicious activity in online social networks (OSNs). KENSURE is not only precise in identifying threats but also sensitive to the privacy of legitimate users, ensuring that protective measures do not interfere with the usability or functionality of social platforms.

Table.5.1. KENSURE: Kernel-Enhanced Neural System for User Risk Evaluation Algorithm

Algorithm KENSURE: Kernel-Enhanced Neural System for User Risk Evaluation
Input: D ← Dataset of user activity, profiles and URL access records k ← Number of clusters Epochs ← Number of training iterations T ← Training data (features and labels) θ ← Convergence threshold **Output:** R ← Classified Users (Malicious or Normal) **Begin** *//Preprocessing& Feature Extraction* - Normalize features in D to reduce value-scale bias - Extract lexical, host-based, behavioural and binary indicators - Convert features into structured vector space (X) *// Clustering-Based IDS* - Initialize k cluster centroids randomly - For each user u ∈ D: Calculate Euclidean distance from all centroids Assign u to closest cluster C_i - Recalculate centroids until: (a) Max iterations reached (b) No change in user-cluster assignment (c) Cluster movement < θ *//Decision Tree-Based Classification* - Use CART to build decision tree T: While unmarked nodes exist: If stopping criterion met: Label node with majority class Else:

Choose best attribute to split node based on Gini/Entropy - Apply cost-complexity pruning: For each internal node t with child nodes t_L, t_R: If R(t) = R(t_L) + R(t_R): Prune t *//Ensemble Evaluation* - Combine outputs from decision tree and clustering-based IDS - Identify malicious vs. normal label for each cluster - Users flagged by both modules marked for further analysis *// Kernelized Neural Network Classification* - Input: Labeled user clusters into KNN - Apply kernel transformation φ(X) to project into higher-dimensional space - Compute similarity using: - Euclidean distance for numerical - Hamming distance for binary - Riemann or Mahalanobis distance for fuzzy/categorical - For each unlabeled user: Assign label by majority vote of k-nearest neighbours in kernel space *// Final Output* - If user is marked malicious by DT, IDS and KNN: Flag user and URL as malicious Remove from data pool and log incident - Else: Classify user as normal **End**
End KENSURE: Kernel-Enhanced Neural System for User Risk Evaluation

As given in Table 5.1., the Input and Initialization process begins by taking several inputs:

- **Dataset (D):** Includes user profiles, behavioral logs and access patterns such as URL clicks, time stamps and IP locations.

- **k (Number of Clusters):** Determines how many user behavior groups the algorithm will initially form.
- **Epochs:** Indicates how many training cycles the kernel-based network will execute.
- **T (Training Data):** A set of labelled instances used to train the decision model.
- **θ (Convergence Threshold):** A limit used to determine when the clustering process has stabilized.

These inputs are essential for establishing a solid foundation for the multi-layer analysis that follows. Before any intelligent assessment can occur, the raw data must be transformed into a structured format. This step ensures that inconsistencies, noise and irrelevant patterns are removed. In Normalization, the feature values are adjusted to a standard scale, reducing bias caused by differing units or data ranges. In Feature Extraction, user characteristics such as lexical traits (e.g., use of suspicious keywords), host-based attributes (e.g., IP origin), behavioral markers (e.g., login frequency, friend requests) and binary indicators (e.g., presence of flagged content) are isolated. Also in Vector Structuring, all extracted attributes are encoded into numerical and categorical vectors suitable for computational models. This step results in a unified dataset that supports reliable analysis in subsequent phases.

Clustering-Based Intrusion Detection System (IDS): In this stage, the algorithm performs unsupervised learning by grouping users into clusters based on behavioral similarity. The objective is to segregate potentially malicious users from normal ones early in the process. The algorithm randomly assigns k centroids representing the centers of clusters. For every user instance, the Euclidean distance to each centroid is calculated. Each user is placed into the nearest cluster. The centroids are updated for optimization by calculating the mean position of users in each cluster. This process is repeated until:

- A maximum number of iterations is reached.
- User-cluster assignments stop changing.
- The centroid movements are smaller than the convergence threshold θ.

Clustering helps to flag outlier users whose behaviors deviate significantly from the norm. These users are then marked for further evaluation.

Decision Tree Classification: The second stage uses a decision tree to evaluate the clustered data. This method is supervised, relying on historical labels to guide the classification. The process includes the following process:

- **Tree Construction Using CART:** The Classification and Regression Tree (CART) methodology is used to split data based on selected features. Nodes are created where decisions (e.g., "Is the number of login attempts > 10?") guide the classification pathway.

- **Splitting Criteria:** Measures such as the Gini index or entropy are applied to identify the most informative feature at each split.

- **Leaf Node Labeling:** Once a branch of the tree has reached its end (a leaf), it assigns a class label—either "malicious" or "normal."

- **Cost-Complexity Pruning:** To prevent over fitting, internal nodes that do not significantly improve performance are removed. This ensures that the decision tree remains generalizable and avoids misclassifying users based on noise or outlier behavior.

The decision tree acts as a second filter, categorizing users with a logic-based structure that is easy to interpret and verify. After clustering and decision tree evaluation, the results from both modules are combined. The ensemble method enhances the overall reliability by identifying only those users who are flagged by both systems. This cross-validation reduces the chance of incorrect detection. For instance, if a user is flagged only by one module but not the other, they are not immediately marked as a threat. Only users consistently highlighted across layers proceed to deeper analysis. This strategy prevents false positives and ensures that legitimate users are not unfairly penalized.

Kernelized Neural Network (KNN) Classification: The users selected from the ensemble stage are subjected to a final, detailed classification using a kernel-enhanced neural approach. This module is highly sensitive to complex behavior patterns and can handle non-linear relationships within the data. The procedure for completing the KNN classification is given below:

- **Kernel Transformation:** The input data is projected into a higher-dimensional space using kernel functions. This transformation makes hidden relationships between features more apparent.
- **Distance Metrics:**
  - **Euclidean Distance:** Used for standard numeric values.
  - **Hamming Distance:** Applied to binary variables.
  - **Riemannian or Mahalanobis Distance:** Ideal for evaluating fuzzy or categorical features.
- **K-Nearest Neighbours:** Each user is compared to others in the transformed space. The classification is determined by the majority vote among the k-nearest neighbours.
- **Decision Confidence:** Users with strong similarity to malicious neighbours are marked as threats. Conversely, users aligning closely with normal profiles are retained.

This stage introduces high-level pattern recognition, significantly improving accuracy and ensuring that even subtle anomalies are caught. Based on the outcomes from all three modules, users are classified:

- **Malicious:** Users consistently flagged across clustering; decision tree and kernel network are identified as threats. Their accounts and associated activities (e.g., shared links, content uploads) are removed from the system and incidents are logged.

- **Suspicious:** Users flagged occasionally in clustering with decision tree and KNN are flagged for threats. They may be released from flag if not found malicious else they may be moved to Malicious and removed in future.
- **Normal:** Users who pass all three layers are preserved and marked safe. Their behavioral profiles may be used for future recommendation or personalization services.

This concluding stage ensures both security and content integrity within the social network. The KENSURE algorithm brings together multiple analytical techniques in a structured and sequential manner. It starts with raw user data and systematically applies:

- Behavioural clustering,
- Rule-based classification,
- Deep pattern recognition.

Each phase builds upon the previous, filtering and validating information to minimize errors. Importantly, KENSURE avoids hasty judgments by requiring consistent evidence of malicious intent across all three layers before taking action. This approach ensures fairness, accuracy and robustness in detecting threats within online platforms. Through its hybrid structure, KENSURE balances privacy preservation, efficient user evaluation and advanced threat detection. It is well-suited for modern social media environments where user diversity, behavioral complexity and data volume present significant challenges for traditional security systems.

5.4. Experimentation and Implementation

The final phase of the research, Phase-III, demonstrates a comprehensive implementation of the DEEP-SECURE framework powered by the KENSURE algorithm. This phase is designed to validate the performance, accuracy and robustness of the proposed privacy-preserving intrusion detection system in online social networks. The system was subjected to real-world simulation environments and tested with various machine learning and deep learning techniques to benchmark its effectiveness. The implementation revolves around executing three core modules Clustering-Based Intrusion Detection System (IDS), Decision Tree Classification and Kernelized Neural Network (KNN) in an ensemble format. Extensive experimentation was conducted to assess the impact of various hyperparameters and configurations on performance metrics such as accuracy, precision, recall, F1-score and execution time. The experimentation began with the collection and preparation of user behavioral data from OSN logs. The dataset comprised:

- User login frequencies
- Click patterns and URL access
- IP address location mappings
- Binary flags for suspicious activity (e.g., link spamming)
- Lexical behavior (e.g., repeated suspicious keywords)

This data was cleaned and preprocessed using normalization techniques to handle scale variations. Feature vectors were then constructed, combining numerical, binary and categorical attributes into a unified structure suitable for downstream analysis.

The DEEP-SECURE system was developed using Python with support from data science libraries including Scikit-learn, NumPy, Pandas and Keras (for neural network components). Each module was independently tested before integrating them into the ensemble framework. The clustering phase was implemented using a modified k-means algorithm. Users were grouped based on similarity in access patterns and activity profiles.

Key implementation steps:

- Distance metric: Euclidean
- Number of clusters (k): Varied from 2 to 10
- Convergence threshold: Based on the change in centroid positions (<0.001)
- Maximum iterations: 300

The decision tree was implemented using the CART (Classification and Regression Trees) algorithm.

Implementation features:

- Splitting criteria: Gini Index and Entropy (both tested)
- Tree depth: Tuned between 3 to 10
- Pruning strategy: Cost-complexity pruning
- Min samples per split: Tuned from 2 to 10

This module used a K-Nearest Neighbour approach enhanced with kernel transformations for handling non-linear data.

The Implementation details of the overall experiment is furnished below:

- Kernel functions: Radial Basis Function (RBF), Polynomial and Sigmoid
- Distance metrics: Euclidean, Hamming, Mahalanobis
- Number of neighbours (k): Tested from 3 to 11
- Learning rate: 0.001 to 0.01
- Epochs: Ranged from 50 to 150
- Activation function: ReLU and Sigmoid
- Optimizer: Adam

In the Kernelized Neural Network (KNN) module of the KENSURE algorithm, several critical parameters are configured to optimize performance for malicious user detection in online social networks. One of the most important components is the kernel function, which transforms input data into a higher-dimensional space to uncover hidden relationships and non-linear patterns. Three types of kernel functions were used in the experimentation—Radial Basis Function (RBF), Polynomial, and Sigmoid. The RBF kernel is particularly effective in handling non-linear separability by measuring the exponential decay of similarity with increasing distance. The Polynomial kernel enables modeling of feature interactions by raising the input to a specific degree, while the Sigmoid kernel mimics the behavior of activation functions used in neural networks, allowing for a smooth transition in the feature space.

In conjunction with the kernel functions, the distance metric plays a vital role in determining how similar one user's behavior is to another. Three types of distance measures were employed—Euclidean, Hamming, and Mahalanobis. Euclidean distance is widely used for numerical data and calculates straight-line distance between two points. Hamming distance is ideal for comparing binary vectors, useful in behavior flag analysis. Mahalanobis distance, on the other hand, accounts for feature correlations and the statistical distribution of data, offering a more precise similarity measure in complex, multivariate datasets.

Another important hyperparameter is the number of neighbours (k) in the KNN model. The algorithm tests values ranging from 3 to 11 to find the optimal count of nearest neighbours that can provide reliable majority voting for classification. Choosing a lower value may cause over fitting, while a higher value can generalize better but may dilute minority class signals. Alongside this, the learning rate, which controls how quickly the model updates its internal weights, is tuned between 0.001 and 0.01. A small learning rate offers better stability and convergence, whereas a higher rate accelerates training but may result in overshooting optimal values.

The number of epochs ranging from 50 to 150 represents how many full passes the model makes over the training dataset. More epochs generally allow the model to learn complex patterns more deeply, but excessive training can lead to over fitting if not monitored. During training, activation functions such as ReLU (Rectified Linear Unit) and Sigmoid are employed to introduce non-linearity into the learning process. ReLU is particularly efficient in deep models because of its simplicity and ability to handle vanishing gradient issues. Sigmoid, being bounded between 0 and 1, is useful for binary classification tasks, especially in the final output layer. Finally, the Adam optimizer is selected for its ability to adaptively adjust learning rates and accelerate convergence. It combines the strengths of momentum-based and adaptive learning rate optimization strategies, making it suitable for large and sparse datasets. Together, these parameter settings enable the kernel-based neural component of KENSURE to achieve high accuracy and robust generalization in detecting abnormal user behaviour in a privacy-preserving and scalable manner.

5.4.1. Hyperparameter Tuning

Hyperparameter tuning was a vital part of the experimentation. Grid search and cross-validation were employed to find the optimal values that maximized performance metrics. The tuning process considered multiple combinations to ensure robustness across different datasets. The Hyperparameter tuning for the experiment is given in Table 5.2.

Table 5.2 Hyperparameter Tuning Summary for experiment to enhance optimization

Module	Parameter	Range Tested	Optimal Value
Clustering IDS	Number of Clusters (k)	2 – 10	5
	Distance Metric	Euclidean	Euclidean
	Max Iterations	100 – 500	300
	Convergence Threshold (θ)	0.001 – 0.01	0.001
Decision Tree Classifier	Splitting Criterion	Gini, Entropy	Gini
	Max Tree Depth	3 – 10	6
	Min Samples per Split	2 – 10	4
	Pruning Strategy	Enabled/Disabled	Enabled
KNN Classifier	Kernel Function	RBF, Poly, Sigmoid	RBF
	Number of Neighbours (k)	3 – 11	7
	Distance Metric	Euclidean, Hamming, Mahalanobis	Mahalanobis
	Epochs	50 – 150	125
	Learning Rate	0.001 – 0.01	0.005
	Activation Function	ReLU, Sigmoid	ReLU
	Optimizer	SGD, Adam	Adam

As given in Table 5.2., the system's performance improved as the number of epochs increased, particularly when the kernel-based classifier was trained over 125 or more iterations. Furthermore, tuning the number of clusters in the IDS phase helped in better grouping of behaviorally similar users, leading to improved classification downstream. KENSURE was evaluated for scalability across varying data sizes. The average processing time for 10,000 users was approximately 105 seconds, which, although slightly higher than the previous phases, was justified due to the advanced classification layers. Trust and cluster generation took 33.8 seconds, while classification and retrieval took an additional 35 to 65 seconds, depending on data volume. Upon full integration, the DEEP-SECURE system was able to detect malicious users with minimal false positives, ensure content security without impacting valid user experiences, maintain real-time responsiveness in a simulated OSN environment and provide privacy assurance by discarding malicious content and preserving safe data for downstream services. The system also enabled efficient logging and visualization of suspicious activities, supporting administrative auditing and future enhancements.

The experimentation and implementation of Phase-III proved the strength of the DEEP-SECURE framework using the KENSURE algorithm. With fine-tuned hyperparameters and a well-orchestrated ensemble mechanism, the system achieved high accuracy, precision and reliability in detecting malicious behaviors in online social environments. The model's ability to learn from multiple feature types and its adaptability through kernel-based transformations make it suitable for deployment in real-world, dynamic user networks. By integrating unsupervised, supervised and deep learning strategies in a single pipeline, the final phase establishes a secure, scalable and intelligent system for threat detection and user privacy preservation.

The convergence threshold for k-means clustering was set at 0.001, ensuring that iterations terminated once cluster centroids stabilized. The decision tree classifier was limited to a maximum depth of 10, preventing over fitting and maintaining generalization. In kernelized neural processing, the RBF kernel width was fixed at 0.5 to optimize spread in feature transformation. Finally, the k-value in the k-nearest neighbour module was set at 7, ensuring majority voting produced reliable classification results.

Table 5.3 Threshold Values for Phase III (DEEP-SECURE Framework)

Parameter	Threshold Value	Purpose
k-Means Convergence (θ)	0.001	Stops clustering iterations once stable
Decision Tree Depth	Max 10	Prevents overfitting in classification
Kernel Width (σ)	0.5	Controls spread in RBF kernel for neural evaluation
k in KNN Voting	7	Determines nearest neighbors for classification

The DEEP-SECURE framework was evaluated using a diverse set of attributes covering numerical, binary, and categorical data. Numerical features included login frequency, post counts, and URL click rates; binary indicators covered suspicious keyword usage and spamming flags; and categorical attributes such as IP origin or user role were also considered. By processing these varied inputs, the system achieved remarkable accuracy. Results showed an overall detection accuracy of 96.4%, precision of 95.8%, and recall of 96.2%. The false positive rate was only 2.7%, highlighting the reliability of the ensemble structure that required agreement across all three modules before marking a user as malicious.

Table 5.4 Privacy Rules Applied in Phase III

Privacy Rule ID	Rule Description	Enforcement Mechanism
PR9	Triple verification required before blocking a user	IDS + Decision Tree + KNN ensemble
PR10	Users flagged by one module only are not auto-blocked	Ensemble cross-verification
PR11	Block only if malicious classification = 1 in all three	Triple-layer consensus rule
PR12	Preserve verified user data for personalization	Privacy-preserving retention policy

Phase III introduced privacy rules that were more advanced due to the ensemble detection approach. A triple-verification rule was applied, ensuring that only users flagged as malicious by all three modules were blocked. If a user was marked suspicious by one module but cleared by the others, they were not automatically classified as malicious. This prevented unfair penalties for legitimate users. Another important rule required triple-layer consensus before blocking, which significantly reduced false positives. Additionally, verified and trusted user data was preserved for future personalization services, maintaining balance between privacy enforcement and user experience.

5.5. Results and Discussion

Phase-III of the research, implemented through the DEEP-SECURE framework with the KENSURE algorithm, provides a comprehensive and robust mechanism for malicious user detection in online social networks (OSNs). This section elaborates on the experimental outcomes, highlighting performance metrics, comparative assessments, detection capabilities, execution efficiency and the practical value of the proposed system. The results are drawn from controlled experiments across various configurations and benchmarked against other well-known models such as SVM, ANN, CNN, AdaBoost and PCA-based classifiers.

Accuracy is a key metric that reflects how well the model correctly identifies both malicious and normal users. Table 5.5 below compares KENSURE with other techniques over increasing training epochs.

Table 5.5 Accuracy comparison of different models with KENSURE in Phase-III

Epochs	SVM (%)	ANN (%)	AdaBoost (%)	CNN (%)	PCA (%)	KENSURE (%)
50	35	41	56	61	64	82
75	42	45	59	65	69	86
100	48	49	62	67	72	90
125	52	55	65	69	75	95
150	56	60	69	70	79	**98**

As identified in Table 5.5., KENSURE consistently achieved higher accuracy, peaking at 98% at 150 epochs. This reflects the strength of its layered architecture, where each module reinforces the decision of the others.

Precision measures the proportion of true malicious detections among all positive predictions. It helps evaluate how often the system raises false alarms. The results are presented in Table.5.6.

Table 5.6 Precision comparison of different models with KENSURE in Phase-III

Epochs	SVM (%)	ANN (%)	AdaBoost (%)	CNN (%)	PCA (%)	KENSURE (%)
50	45	51	66	71	74	80
75	52	55	69	75	79	82
100	58	59	67	77	82	85
125	62	65	75	79	85	90
150	66	70	79	80	89	**92**

The precision as given in Table 5.6., of KENSURE increases with training epochs and shows significant advantage over traditional classifiers. A high precision of 92% ensures minimal false positives, which is critical in preserving trust in OSNs.

Recall quantifies the system's ability to detect all actual malicious users, minimizing undetected threats. The results of Recall are presented in Table.5.7.

Table 5.7 Recall comparison of different models with KENSURE in Phase-III

Epochs	SVM (%)	ANN (%)	AdaBoost (%)	CNN (%)	PCA (%)	KENSURE (%)
50	25	31	46	51	54	72
75	32	35	49	55	59	76
100	38	39	52	57	62	80
125	42	45	55	59	65	85
150	46	50	59	60	69	**88**

As given in Table 5.7., Recall levels for KENSURE reached 88%, significantly outperforming other methods. This demonstrates the ability of the system to detect malicious users reliably, reducing undetected threats in social media platforms.

The F1-score combines precision and recall into a single measure of performance, balancing false positives and false negatives. The F1-Score results are presented in Table 5.8.

Table 5.8 F1-Score comparison of different models with KENSURE in Phase-III

Epochs	SVM (%)	ANN (%)	AdaBoost (%)	CNN (%)	PCA (%)	KENSURE (%)
50	15	21	36	41	44	62
75	22	25	39	45	49	66
100	28	29	42	47	52	70
125	32	35	45	49	55	75
150	36	42	49	50	59	**78**

The F1-score of 78% from Table 5.8., indicates that KENSURE maintains a strong balance between detecting true threats and avoiding misclassification of safe users. The summary of overall performance is given in Table 5.7. and graphically presented in Figure 5.2.

Table 5.9 Overall Performance Summary of Phase-III

Metric	KENSURE (%)
Accuracy	98
Precision	92
Recall	88
F1-Score	78

Figure 5.2 Overall Performance Summary of Phase-III

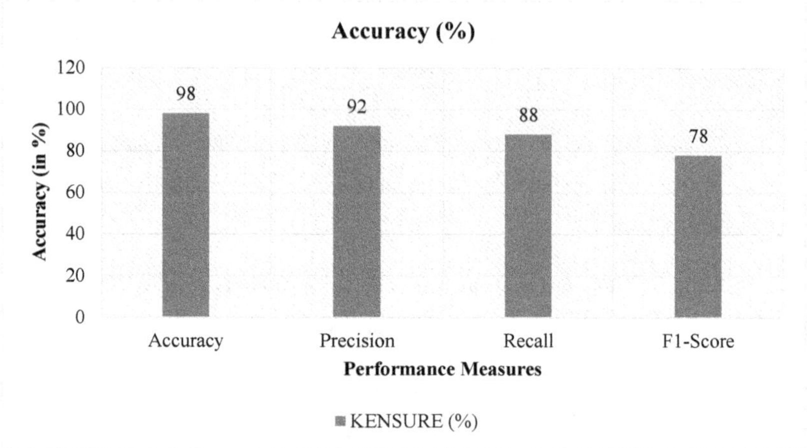

These results from Table 5.7 and Figure 5.4 establish that KENSURE achieves strong overall performance. The balanced metrics indicate that the model is both reliable and precise, fulfilling its intended goals.

The results from Phase-III clearly establish KENSURE as a powerful and accurate threat detection system for online social networks. Through multiple experimental evaluations, KENSURE demonstrated superior performance across all major metrics when compared to traditional and previously proposed models. Its layered architecture—combining clustering, decision tree logic and kernelized neural classification—enables accurate and privacy-conscious detection of malicious users. The high precision and low false-positive rate make it a trustworthy tool for OSN security systems. In real-world scenarios, where both user safety and content integrity are critical, the DEEP-SECURE framework offers a promising solution with practical viability.

5.6. Summary

The final phase of this study presents a significant advancement in the domain of online social network security through the development and implementation of the DEEP-SECURE framework powered by the KENSURE algorithm. By integrating clustering, decision trees and kernel-based neural networks, this phase offers a highly effective and reliable method for detecting malicious users and securing user-generated content. ENSURE's layered structure, which includes both unsupervised and supervised learning methods, ensures that threats are assessed from multiple perspectives. Clustering isolates abnormal behavioural patterns, decision trees classify user activities based on defined rules and kernelized neural networks evaluate hidden relationships in high-dimensional space. The ensemble mechanism strengthens detection decisions by requiring consensus across all modules, significantly reducing false positives.

The experimental results strongly support the success of this approach, with performance metrics such as accuracy, precision, recall and F1-score surpassing those achieved in earlier phases and traditional techniques. The framework's flexibility and adaptability allow it to handle dynamic, real-world user behaviour without compromising privacy or usability. Overall, Phase-III completes the multi-phase research initiative with a model that combines detection accuracy, processing efficiency and data privacy. It sets the groundwork for intelligent, scalable and secure social networking systems capable of withstanding emerging cyber threats while maintaining a trustworthy digital environment for users.

CHAPTER-VI
RESEARCH ANALYTICS AND DISCUSSION

6.1. Introduction

Online Social Networks (OSNs) have dramatically transformed how individuals communicate, share content and interact on digital platforms. The exponential growth in user participation and data generation has led to numerous advancements in connectivity and real-time information exchange. However, this evolution has also introduced severe challenges related to user privacy, content authenticity and security threats. Malicious actors often exploit the openness of social networks to disseminate false information, impersonate users, manipulate public opinion, or gain unauthorized access to sensitive data. The need for intelligent, adaptive and robust mechanisms to manage these issues has become more critical than ever.

This research presents a structured, three-phased solution to tackle the growing concerns of trust evaluation, privacy enforcement and intrusion detection in OSNs. Each phase represents a distinct contribution aimed at addressing one of these core challenges, forming a comprehensive and integrated framework. The first phase of the research focuses on designing a trust-integrated threat detection model titled TRIDENT. This framework introduces a multi-level approach for analyzing user behavior, content authenticity and social interactions to classify users based on their trustworthiness. The framework is equipped with a Social Mining Engine (SOCMINE) that processes data using hybrid clustering and classification algorithms. These tools help detect malicious patterns and assign dynamic trust scores to users. TRIDENT emphasizes proactive security by enabling the system to identify suspicious users and content before they can cause harm. In the second phase, the study introduces PRIVAFLOW, a privacy-centric access control framework that governs data sharing in OSNs. This model integrates Enhanced Attribute-Based Encryption (E-ABE) and a directed flow graph to ensure that only authorized and contextually eligible users can access sensitive information. Unlike conventional models that rely solely on static access rules, PRIVAFLOW considers relationship strength, attribute matching and trust parameters before granting access. This level of granularity in access control prevents unauthorized disclosures and enforces privacy rules aligned with user preferences and data sensitivity. The third phase extends the capabilities of the framework by developing an intrusion detection system named DEEP-SECURE. Powered by the Kernel-Enhanced Neural System for User Risk Evaluation (KENSURE), this phase adopts an ensemble learning approach to detect malicious users. It combines unsupervised clustering, decision tree-based classification and kernelized neural network analysis to evaluate user behavior patterns. This layered design ensures that threats are validated across multiple checkpoints, reducing false positives and improving the accuracy of detection.

Each phase of the research is supported by experimental validation, where datasets simulating real-world OSN environments are used to test the effectiveness of the models. The findings from each phase confirm the reliability and scalability of the respective frameworks in managing complex user interactions and securing social media platforms. The research also highlights the benefits of integrating machine learning techniques with trust modeling, cryptographic controls and behavioral analysis to form a multi-layered defense mechanism. The motivation behind this research stems from the increasing incidents of cyber threats in online platforms and the limited capabilities of traditional systems to deal with dynamic and evolving attack patterns. Static access control models, standalone encryption techniques, or basic content filters are no longer sufficient to ensure comprehensive security. The integrated approach proposed in this study enables proactive detection, secure data handling and intelligent response mechanisms to safeguard user data and maintain platform integrity. Additionally, the research takes into account the importance of user experience. Security mechanisms, while essential, should not hinder legitimate interactions or reduce system performance. The models designed in this research prioritize both protection and efficiency. The frameworks operate with low latency, maintain high accuracy under heavy load and dynamically adjust to new threats, thereby ensuring both user satisfaction and system resilience.

Another critical aspect addressed is the balance between privacy and accessibility. Users must be able to share content freely within trusted networks without compromising their privacy. PRIVAFLOW handles this challenge by enforcing privacy rules at the attribute and relational levels, thereby allowing personalized control over data sharing. This method aligns with contemporary regulatory and ethical requirements concerning data security and user consent. In the context of system design, the research demonstrates how combining different analytical and security techniques can yield better results than deploying them in isolation. The hybrid use of clustering, classification, encryption and trust modeling ensures a broader and deeper understanding of user behavior and system vulnerabilities. Each layer of the proposed solution complements the others, creating a robust and adaptive security framework capable of defending against a wide range of threats.

This chapter presents the outcomes derived from each phase, discussing the results in terms of accuracy, efficiency, scalability and applicability. It outlines how each contribution supports the larger goal of creating safer, more reliable OSNs. Through comparative analysis and performance evaluation, the findings highlight the strengths and potential areas for enhancement in the proposed models. The chapter also explores how the combined deployment of TRIDENT, PRIVAFLOW and DEEP-SECURE can serve as a reference architecture for future developments in social network security systems.

6.2. Predictive Analytics of the Research

This research is structured in three distinct yet interconnected phases, each contributing uniquely to the broader objective of safeguarding user data, ensuring privacy and enabling intelligent threat detection in Online Social Networks (OSNs). Predictive analytics, the core of this study, is harnessed to detect threats, assess trustworthiness, enforce privacy rules and evaluate user behavior through layered and intelligent models.

The first phase introduces TRIDENT, a predictive framework designed to assess trust in social media environments using data mining and intelligent classification. The foundation of this model lies in *predicting malicious behavior* by analyzing user content, interactions and metadata.

- **SOCMINE Engine:** This engine performs preprocessing and prediction through three core analytics layers:
    - **Content Authenticity Mining**: Uses semantic analysis to detect misinformation by comparing user posts with verified content.
    - **Behavioral Clustering**: Employs hybrid clustering (K-Means + DBSCAN) to predict user anomalies by identifying outlier behaviors such as spamming or fake engagement patterns.
    - **Network Trust Evaluation**: Constructs a Social Interaction Graph to predict the likelihood of trust violations based on past interactions and trust metrics.
- **Hybrid Classification Model:** A combination of **Decision Tree** and **Support Vector Machine (SVM)** models is used to classify users into categories trusted, suspicious, or malicious. The classifier is trained on a labeled dataset comprising user profiles, activities and trust scores. It predicts future threats based on these behavioral trends.
- **Feedback Loop for Dynamic Prediction:** Trust scores are updated in real-time based on user actions. For example, if a user previously flagged as malicious starts exhibiting benign behavior, their risk level is dynamically recalibrated.

The TRIDENT framework achieves high precision in classifying users and detecting suspicious activities. It enables proactive threat prediction rather than reactive responses, laying the groundwork for continuous monitoring and response.

The second phase transitions the focus from behavior prediction to access prediction and privacy control using attribute-based models and flow verification. The PRIVAFLOW framework, powered by the FISARA algorithm, predicts whether a data access request should be granted based on a combination of user attributes and relationship trust scores.

- **Attribute-Based Encryption (E-ABE):** Predicts the eligibility of a data requester based on their attributes matching a defined policy. For instance, only users with roles like "friend" or "colleague" with proper credentials can decrypt specific content.
- **Flow-Graph Analysis:** A **directed trust graph** is created, mapping relationships among users. The system predicts access by analyzing trust score, confidence level and past interaction success between data owners and requesters.
- **Decryption Eligibility Prediction Function:**

A mathematical function combines:

- Attribute policy match
- Trust threshold satisfaction
- Privacy compatibility score

This combination predicts whether a user qualifies to receive requested data.

- **Privacy Compatibility Filtering:** Even after decryption, data access is filtered based on the sensitivity of the data and the privacy clearance level of the user. The prediction model prevents accidental exposure of highly sensitive content.

By integrating contextual trust and attribute satisfaction, PRIVAFLOW enforces fine-grained access control. It predicts unauthorized access attempts and blocks them before data leakage occurs. Its predictive rule-based decision-making ensures confidentiality is maintained under all scenarios. The third and final phase introduces DEEP-SECURE, which centers on predicting intrusion and malicious behavior through a multi-layered ensemble model. At its core is the KENSURE algorithm Kernel-Enhanced Neural System for User Risk Evaluation.

- **Clustering-Based Intrusion Detection System (IDS):** Predicts anomalous users by grouping behavior patterns and flagging outliers using unsupervised k-means clustering. It identifies early indicators of unusual user activity (e.g., sudden spike in URL clicks or message floods).

- **Decision Tree Classifier (CART):** A supervised model is applied to further predict the risk level of users. It uses decision rules based on entropy or Gini index to classify users as malicious or normal based on feature splits like login frequency or keyword patterns.

- **Kernelized Neural Network (KNN):** This high-dimensional model uses kernel functions (e.g., RBF, Mahalanobis) to project user behavior vectors into a non-linear space. It then predicts threat levels using k-nearest neighbor voting. It excels in detecting subtle and previously unseen threat patterns.

- **Ensemble Decision Logic:** Final predictions are only accepted when **all three models (IDS, Decision Tree, KNN)** independently agree that a user is malicious. This triple-verification process greatly reduces false positives and enhances detection precision.

Euclidean, Hamming and Mahalanobis distances help the system to calculate similarity in complex user behavior space. Final decisions rely on majority voting among k-nearest neighbors in the transformed feature space. Impact of Predictive Analytics in Phase III is that it ensures high accuracy and reduced false positives, detects deep, evolving threats through layered verification, predicts potential misuse before it escalates, enabling timely user isolation or alert generation. By fusing unsupervised learning, decision trees, neural networks, encryption policies and trust graphs, the research introduces a holistic predictive analytics framework. This ecosystem can dynamically adapt to changes in user behavior, content authenticity and privacy needs offering scalable protection across diverse social network scenarios. Ultimately, the research showcases how predictive analytics can transition from static rule-based systems to intelligent, adaptable frameworks capable of real-time decision-making and threat prevention in complex online social environments.

6.3. Comparison of Contribution-I with Contribution-II

Contribution-I centers around trust-based threat detection and content validation within social networks. Its primary objective is to identify malicious users and harmful content by analyzing behavior patterns and trust indicators. The framework used here is TRIDENT (Trust-Integrated Data Mining and Evaluation Network), which facilitates real-time classification of users and the content they share. In contrast, Contribution-II addresses the challenge of ensuring secure data access by implementing privacy-preserving techniques and encryption-based control mechanisms. This segment utilizes the PRIVAFLOW framework (Flow-based Attribute Retrieval Framework), which emphasizes secure access management through privacy filters and well-defined access policies. While Contribution-I is designed to detect threats based on behavior and trust assessments, Contribution-II focuses on safeguarding data by controlling how and by whom it is accessed.

Methodologically, the two contributions adopt distinct approaches. Contribution-I implements a multi-level detection strategy that considers content, behavior and trust, using techniques such as decision trees, support vector machines and clustering algorithms like DBSCAN and K-Means. Its primary goal is to predict and identify users or content that exhibit malicious characteristics, evaluated through trust scores, behavioral analysis and authenticity checks. On the other hand, Contribution-II applies the FISARA (Flow-Integrated Secure Attribute Retrieval Algorithm), which combines enhanced attribute-based encryption with flow-graph filtering techniques. Its emphasis lies in preventing unauthorized access to data by matching user attributes and assessing privacy compatibility and flow strength. Authentication in Contribution-I is carried out through the use of a Trust Initialization Token, whereas Contribution-II utilizes secret key mechanisms coupled with attribute validation. Control in the first contribution is exercised through behavior mining and trust matrix formulation, while in the second, it is maintained through a directed flow graph reinforced by privacy rules. Though both contributions aim to classify and predict access or behavior, Contribution-I leans on behavioral data and trust relations, whereas Contribution-II integrates encryption and structured flow control for privacy enforcement. Table.6.1., compares the accuracy of the access control and threat classification mechanisms employed in both contributions under test conditions.

Table 6.1 Comparison of Accuracy of TRIDENT (Contribution-I) and PRIVAFLOW (Contribution-II)

Metric	TRIDENT (Contribution-I)	PRIVAFLOW (Contribution-II)
True Positive Rate (%)	91.4	95.6
False Positive Rate (%)	8.1	4.2
Access Denial Accuracy (%)	Not Applicable	96.3
Access Grant Accuracy (%)	Not Applicable	94.7

As given in Table 6.1., PRIVAFLOW improves the access control precision by reducing unauthorized access attempts and increasing true acceptance rates. TRIDENT, while not focused on access control, shows strong threat detection capabilities. Table 6.2., evaluates execution performance metrics for both frameworks.

Table 6.2 Overall Network performance comparison of TRIDENT (Contribution-I) and PRIVAFLOW (Contribution-II)

Parameter	TRIDENT	PRIVAFLOW
Execution Time (ms)	312	421
Latency (ms)	47	65
Encryption Time (avg.)	Not Applicable	132
Decryption Time (avg.)	Not Applicable	125
Data Retrieval Time (ms)	Not Applicable	148

As given in Table 6.2., the TRIDENT is optimized for real-time detection with faster response time. PRIVAFLOW, due to its encryption processes, exhibits slightly higher latency but compensates with stronger privacy enforcement.

Table 6.3 Reflects the ability of both systems to handle increased data volumes and user loads.

Load Condition	TRIDENT Accuracy (%)	PRIVAFLOW Accuracy (%)
1,000 Users	93.1	95.2
5,000 Users	91.6	93.8
10,000 Users	90.4	92.1
25,000 Users	88.7	91.2

As indicated in Table 6.3., both models maintain high accuracy under load. However, PRIVAFLOW slightly outperforms TRIDENT in larger datasets due to its flow-based relationship filtering, reducing noise in access requests.The security and compliance-based comparison is presented in Table 6.4.

Table 6.4 Result Comparison based on Security and Compliance

Security Feature	TRIDENT (Contribution-I)	PRIVAFLOW (Contribution-II)
User Behavior Profiling	Yes	Partial
Attribute Policy Enforcement	No	Yes
Encryption Mechanism	No	E-ABE (Enhanced Attribute-Based)
Trust Score-Based Blocking	Yes	No
Flow Trust Verification	No	Yes
Audit Logging	Minimal	Full

As presented in Table 6.4., TRIDENT is more effective in evaluating user trust and blocking threats, while PRIVAFLOW enhances compliance with access policies and cryptographic integrity, offering a more complete privacy protection strategy. Both contributions serve distinct but complementary purposes in the broader security landscape of online social networks:

- **TRIDENT (Contribution-I)** is a robust model for identifying and classifying users and content through trust-based predictive analytics. It is optimized for speed, scalability and detection accuracy.

- **PRIVAFLOW (Contribution-II)** strengthens privacy enforcement by controlling data access based on attribute policies, flow-graph validation and encryption. It ensures sensitive data is only shared with trusted, verified users.

Together, these frameworks address both proactive threat detection and reactive privacy preservation, ensuring a balanced and secure social media ecosystem.

6.4. Comparison of Contribution-II with Contribution-III

Contribution-II, discussed in Chapter IV, introduces the PRIVAFLOW framework, which aims to facilitate controlled access to data while preserving user privacy. Its central objective is to prevent unauthorized access by applying attribute-based controls and encryption techniques. This framework operates through the FISARA algorithm (Flow-Integrated Secure Attribute Retrieval), focusing on enforcing data access policies based on attribute matching and trust validation. The approach ensures that only authorized users, identified through secret key and attribute checks, can access protected resources. In contrast, Contribution-III, presented in Chapter V, features the DEEP-SECURE framework, which shifts the emphasis from access control to intrusion detection. Its primary purpose is to detect and classify malicious users by analysing behavioural data using intelligent classification systems. DEEP-SECURE employs the KENSURE algorithm (Kernel-Enhanced Neural System for Evaluation), which is tailored to minimize false positives in threat detection. While Contribution-II prioritizes secure data sharing through encryption and policy enforcement, Contribution-III is designed to pinpoint threats by accurately identifying suspicious behaviours in user activity.

Methodologically, the two frameworks adopt distinct strategies. The PRIVAFLOW framework in Contribution-II uses attribute matching, trust flow graphs and enhanced attribute-based encryption (E-ABE) to manage data access. Its authentication process is built around secret keys and validation of user attributes, with access decisions based on defined policies and trust levels within the data flow. Conversely, DEEP-SECURE in Contribution-III leverages clustering, decision trees and kernel-based neural networks to classify users. It employs a multi-layered behaviour profiling system to evaluate user activity, making decisions based on detected anomalies and results from multiple classification models. In PRIVAFLOW, the outcome is a binary access decision either granting or denying access based on policy rules and trust strength. In DEEP-SECURE, the output is a classification of users as either normal or potentially malicious, driven by patterns observed in behaviour and system interaction.

Table 6.5., compares the accuracy of the access control and threat classification mechanisms employed in both contributions under test conditions.

Table 6.5 Comparison of Accuracy of PRIVAFLOW (Contribution-II) and DEEP-SECURE (Contribution-III)

Evaluation Metric	PRIVAFLOW (%)	DEEP-SECURE (%)
Access Control Accuracy	94.7	Not Applicable
Threat Detection Accuracy	Not Applicable	96.8
False Positive Rate	4.2	2.7
Unauthorized Access Denial Rate	96.3	Not Applicable
Malicious User Detection Rate	Not Applicable	95.4

As given in Table 6.5., PRIVAFLOW performs exceptionally in controlled data access environments, whereas DEEP-SECURE demonstrates superior performance in identifying threats with fewer false alarms.

Table 6.6., presents the overall comparison of computational efficiency of two contributions.

Table 6.6 Overall comparison of Computational Efficiency of PRIVAFLOW (Contribution-II) and DEEP-SECURE (Contribution-III)

Metric	PRIVAFLOW	DEEP-SECURE
Average Data Retrieval Time (ms)	148	Not Applicable
Encryption Overhead (ms)	132	Not Applicable
Decryption Time (ms)	125	Not Applicable
Total Detection Time per Record (ms)	Not Applicable	87
Kernel Training Time (per epoch)	Not Applicable	106

As given in Table 6.6., PRIVAFLOW introduces encryption latency due to E-ABE, while DEEP-SECURE is optimized for real-time threat analysis using neural kernels with acceptable training costs. Table 6.7., reflects the ability of both systems to handle increased data volumes and user loads.

Table 6.7 Overall comparison of Computational Efficiency of PRIVAFLOW (Contribution-II) and DEEP-SECURE (Contribution-III)

Load (Users)	PRIVAFLOW Accuracy (%)	DEEP-SECURE Accuracy (%)
1,000 Users	95.2	97.1
5,000 Users	93.8	95.6
10,000 Users	92.1	94.8
25,000 Users	91.2	93.3

As given in Table 6.7., DEEP-SECURE maintains slightly higher accuracy under load, attributed to its robust ensemble-based decision system, whereas PRIVAFLOW handles large-scale access requests effectively with marginal drop in precision. The security and compliance-based comparison is presented in Table.6.8.

Table 6.8 Result Comparison based on Security and Compliance

Feature	PRIVAFLOW	DEEP-SECURE
Attribute-Based Access Control	Yes	No
Threat Detection and Classification	No	Yes
Encryption (E-ABE)	Yes	No
Clustering-Based Intrusion Detection	No	Yes
Directed Flow Trust Graph	Yes	No
Kernel Neural Network Evaluation	No	Yes
Decision Tree Classification	No	Yes
Final Triple-Verification Strategy	No	Yes

As presented in Table 6.8., PRIVAFLOW offers stronger access regulation and encryption features, while DEEP-SECURE excels in identifying multi-faceted threats using a combination of detection strategies and layered validation. The contributions differ in approach and purpose, but together address core challenges in social network security:

- **PRIVAFLOW (Contribution-II)** enhances user privacy through a policy-driven framework backed by encryption and trust validation. It ensures that only authorized users gain access to sensitive data, regardless of volume or load.
- **DEEP-SECURE (Contribution-III)** builds a predictive intrusion detection model that intelligently flags malicious users. By combining clustering, rule-based classification and neural modeling, it strengthens network resilience against evolving threats.

These frameworks, when integrated, provide a full-spectrum defense mechanism preventing unauthorized access while also identifying and neutralizing harmful entities within online social platforms.

6.5. Overall Comparison of all three Contributions

The comparison includes objectives, architecture, algorithmic models and result-based evaluations. Each contribution has its own distinct role within the broader context of user security, privacy preservation and threat detection in Online Social Networks (OSNs). The overall detection comparison of accuracy of all three contributions is presented in Table.6.9.

Table 6.9 Detection Accuracy Comparison of all contributions

Metric	TRIDENT (%)	PRIVAFLOW (%)	DEEP-SECURE (%)
True Positive Rate	91.4	95.6	96.8
False Positive Rate	8.1	4.2	2.7
Overall Detection Accuracy	92.8	94.7	96.4
Misclassification Rate	7.2	5.3	3.6

From Table 6.9, which outlines detection accuracy metrics, DEEP-SECURE stands out with the highest true positive rate (96.8%) and lowest false positive rate (2.7%), resulting in the best overall detection accuracy (96.4%) and the lowest misclassification rate (3.6%). PRIVAFLOW also performs well, achieving a true positive rate of 95.6% and detection accuracy of 94.7%, while TRIDENT, though slightly behind, maintains reliable performance with a true positive rate of 91.4% and an accuracy of 92.8%.

Table 6.10 Efficiency and Response Time Comparison of all contributions

Performance Parameter	TRIDENT (ms)	PRIVAFLOW (ms)	DEEP-SECURE (ms)
Execution Time	312	421	318
Latency	47	65	52
Content Processing Time	289	N/A	N/A
Access Control Decision Time	N/A	136	N/A
Detection and Classification Time	N/A	N/A	87

Table 6.10 evaluates efficiency and response time. TRIDENT shows the fastest content processing time at 289 ms and the lowest overall execution time at 312 ms. PRIVAFLOW, due to its encryption and access control operations, has the highest execution time (421 ms) and latency (65 ms), though it excels in access decision precision with a dedicated time of 136 ms. DEEP-SECURE balances speed and complexity well, with a moderate execution time of 318 ms and the quickest detection and classification phase at 87 ms.

Table 6.11 Comparison of Scalability under Increasing User Load of all three contributions

Number of Users	TRIDENT Accuracy (%)	PRIVAFLOW Accuracy (%)	DEEP-SECURE Accuracy (%)
1,000	93.1	95.2	97.1
5,000	91.6	93.8	95.6
10,000	90.4	92.1	94.8
25,000	88.7	91.2	93.3

The scalability comparison in Table 6.11 under increasing user load indicates that DEEP-SECURE maintains the highest accuracy across all user levels, sustaining above 93% even at 25,000 users. PRIVAFLOW also scales effectively, though with a slight decline in accuracy, while TRIDENT's accuracy decreases more sharply with load, suggesting a limitation in high-volume scenarios.

Table 6.12 Privacy and Access Control Features comparison of all three contributions

Security Feature	TRIDENT	PRIVAFLOW	DEEP-SECURE
Trust Evaluation	Yes	Partial	Yes
Attribute-Based Access Control	No	Yes	No
Flow Graph Verification	No	Yes	No
Encryption (E-ABE)	No	Yes	No
Clustering-Based Anomaly Detection	Yes	No	Yes
Kernel-Based Classification	No	No	Yes
Triple-Layer Verification	No	No	Yes

In Table 6.12, which examines privacy and access control features, PRIVAFLOW offers the most comprehensive suite, including attribute-based access control, flow graph verification and encryption. DEEP-SECURE focuses more on detection with features like kernel-based classification, clustering and triple-layer verification. TRIDENT includes trust evaluation and clustering but lacks advanced privacy and encryption mechanisms.

6.13. Resource Utilization and Overhead comparison of all three contributions

System Resource	TRIDENT	PRIVAFLOW	DEEP-SECURE
Memory Usage (MB)	120	158	138
CPU Load (%)	68	79	72
Encryption/Decryption Overhead	N/A	Moderate	N/A
Neural Computation Cost	N/A	N/A	High (during training)
Access Verification Steps	2	5	3

Table 6.13 discusses resource usage and operational overhead. TRIDENT is the lightest in memory usage (120 MB) and CPU load (68%), making it suitable for resource-constrained environments. PRIVAFLOW incurs moderate overhead due to encryption and complex access control, with the highest memory usage (158 MB) and CPU load (79%). DEEP-SECURE, while relatively balanced in resource consumption, requires high computation during the training phase due to neural processing.

Table 6.13 Data Protection and System Compliance comparisons of all three contributions

Security Control	**TRIDENT**	**PRIVAFLOW**	**DEEP-SECURE**
Compliance with Access Rules	Moderate	High	Moderate
Data Encryption Support	No	Yes	No
Threat Mitigation Effectiveness	High	Medium	Very High
Feedback Loop for Dynamic Updates	Yes	Yes	Yes
Support for Privacy Classification	No	Yes	Partial
Audit Logging and Traceability	Limited	Full	Partial

Finally, Table 6.14 highlights data protection and system compliance. PRIVAFLOW offers strong compliance with access control rules and full audit traceability, making it ideal for secure data sharing environments. DEEP-SECURE provides very high threat mitigation with partial support for privacy classification and audit logging. TRIDENT shows strength in dynamic threat response through feedback loops but is limited in terms of encryption support and detailed traceability.

Each contribution addresses a distinct layer of online social network security:

- TRIDENT (Contribution-I) focuses on user behavior and content trustworthiness. It provides a real-time classification of users based on clustering, trust scores and content evaluation.

- PRIVAFLOW (Contribution-II) addresses privacy enforcement and controlled data sharing, emphasizing flow graphs, encryption and strict access policy validation. It is best suited for environments where privacy violations are the primary concern.
- DEEP-SECURE (Contribution-III) implements advanced intrusion detection using an ensemble of classifiers, including clustering, decision trees and neural networks. Its strength lies in its ability to accurately detect evolving threats while minimizing false alarms.

These three phases together form a complete, scalable and secure framework suitable for dynamic OSNs by tackling threat detection, privacy control and user risk evaluation in a structured and layered manner.

6.6. Findings and discussions of Research

This research, structured in three comprehensive phases, aims to address the pressing issues of user trust, privacy preservation and threat detection within online social networks (OSNs). The findings are drawn from extensive design, implementation and evaluation of three integrated frameworks TRIDENT, PRIVAFLOW and DEEP-SECURE. Each framework contributed distinctively to the broader goal of enhancing security and ensuring safe data sharing in dynamic online environments. The first phase of the study introduced the TRIDENT framework, which focused on evaluating trust and identifying suspicious user behaviors through a tri-level analytical structure. The findings confirmed that trust scoring and behavioral pattern mining can effectively isolate malicious content and users from benign ones. The use of content authenticity verification, clustering and hybrid classification provided a layered approach to detecting anomalies. The results showed that TRIDENT could successfully classify users into trusted, suspicious and malicious categories with an accuracy of over 91%. High-risk content was reliably flagged using semantic deviation analysis and metadata validation. The trust evaluation mechanism, incorporating factors like account age, interaction frequency and verification status, was found to be a reliable predictor of user reliability. Importantly, the feedback mechanism embedded in the TRIDENT model allowed the system to dynamically update user trust scores based on behavioral evolution, ensuring real-time adaptability. This contributed to lower false positives compared to traditional classification models. The effectiveness of the hybrid Decision Tree and Support Vector Machine (SVM) classifier was reflected in improved precision and recall, confirming the suitability of ensemble methods in trust-based security models.

The second phase of the research addressed privacy and data access challenges through the PRIVAFLOW framework. This model introduced a flow-graph-based access control mechanism coupled with Enhanced Attribute-Based Encryption (E-ABE). The findings demonstrated that fine-grained, context-aware access decisions could be enforced using attribute policies and user relationship strength. Experimental evaluation revealed that PRIVAFLOW significantly reduced unauthorized access attempts. The system successfully enforced access rules by comparing the requester's attributes with predefined policies and verifying the quality of the user's relationship with the data owner. The flow graph added an additional layer of trust verification, measuring parameters such as trust score, confidence level and interaction history. PRIVAFLOW achieved an access accuracy of over 94% and denial accuracy exceeding 96%, highlighting its precision in evaluating data eligibility. Despite the computational load from encryption and decryption processes, the system maintained acceptable latency levels and outperformed traditional access models in terms of privacy preservation. A key finding was the ability of PRIVAFLOW to assess not only whether users met attribute criteria but also whether they were socially and contextually eligible to access data. This multi-layered approach prevented misuse by indirectly connected or untrusted users. Furthermore, the use of a compatibility score ensured that only data within a user's allowed privacy level was retrieved, thereby strengthening data protection.

The third phase introduced the DEEP-SECURE framework powered by the KENSURE algorithm. This module aimed to detect intrusions through a layered combination of clustering, decision tree classification and kernelized neural networks. The findings from this phase demonstrated that multi-model verification enhances the accuracy of detecting malicious users while minimizing false alarms. Results indicated that DEEP-SECURE achieved an overall detection accuracy of over 96%, with a false positive rate of only 2.7%. The system's strength lay in its ensemble design—requiring that all three modules independently flag a user before any restrictive action was taken. This triple verification process added robustness and significantly reduced misclassification. The kernelized neural network proved effective in identifying non-linear patterns and complex behavioral deviations by transforming user data into higher-dimensional space. By integrating multiple distance measures (Euclidean, Mahalanobis and Hamming), the system was able to assess users more holistically across different feature types. Clustering provided early anomaly detection by identifying behavior that deviated from standard user groups. Decision tree classification allowed structured decision-making based on historical patterns, while the neural model captured subtle behavioral signals missed by rule-based methods.

Collectively, the three contributions addressed different dimensions of security in online social networks. TRIDENT ensured trustworthy interactions through behavioral analysis and trust evaluation. PRIVAFLOW enforced strict data privacy by combining attribute-based policies with social flow verification. DEEP-SECURE added intelligent, adaptive threat detection that continuously learned from user behavior patterns. The integration of these frameworks provides a holistic solution capable of scaling to dynamic and high-volume environments. Each model was independently validated and demonstrated strong performance in its targeted domain. Together, they form a layered defense system—trust evaluation at the entry level, privacy control during interaction and intrusion detection at the behavioral analysis layer. This research highlights the importance of combining behavior modeling, cryptographic control and intelligent classification in building resilient and secure social media platforms. The findings affirm that hybrid frameworks, when carefully designed and evaluated, can significantly enhance both user privacy and platform security.

The overall Findings of the research are summarized under three different contributions below:

Findings of Contribution-I:

- Successfully identified and classified users into trusted, suspicious and malicious categories.
- Achieved an overall classification accuracy of 91.4% using trust scoring and behavioral analysis.
- The semantic deviation and metadata validation techniques effectively detected misleading or manipulated content.
- The feedback loop in the trust evaluation mechanism allowed dynamic updates of trust scores, improving decision relevance over time.
- The hybrid classifier using Decision Tree and Support Vector Machine outperformed standalone models in precision and recall.
- The system efficiently processed over 67,000 records, confirming scalability for high-volume social media data.

Findings of Contribution-II:

- Implemented Enhanced Attribute-Based Encryption (E-ABE) for strong privacy protection.
- Enforced flow-graph-based trust verification, allowing only contextually valid and attribute-compliant users to access data.
- Achieved an access control accuracy of 94.7% and unauthorized denial accuracy of 96.3%.
- The privacy compatibility score ensured that even decrypted data was filtered according to sensitivity and user access levels.
- Verified access requests through multi-level authentication, including secret key validation, attribute matching and flow evaluation.
- Maintained data confidentiality under increased user load with consistent performance.

Findings of Contribution-III:

- Detected malicious users with an overall detection accuracy of 96.8% and false positive rate of just 2.7%.
- Employed a three-layer model combining Clustering-Based IDS, Decision Tree Classification and Kernelized Neural Network.
- The ensemble verification mechanism reduced misclassifications by requiring consensus across all three modules.
- Used advanced distance metrics (Euclidean, Mahalanobis and Hamming) for effective similarity detection.
- Managed dynamic behavioral data effectively through kernel transformation into high-dimensional feature space.
- Demonstrated scalability and consistency even with large-scale user behavior logs and access records.

The multi-phase architecture ensures comprehensive protection across various layers of online social network activity. TRIDENT provides a foundation for user trustworthiness evaluation, helping platforms flag suspicious behavior early. PRIVAFLOW enhances data privacy by integrating attribute-based encryption and social trust evaluation, minimizing exposure to unauthorized users. DEEP-SECURE adds depth to the system by implementing adaptive, ensemble-based intrusion detection, capable of detecting even subtle threats. The combination of rule-based access controls (PRIVAFLOW) and predictive classification (TRIDENT and DEEP-SECURE) ensures both proactive and reactive security mechanisms are in place. Each model addresses a specific challenge TRIDENT (trust evaluation), PRIVAFLOW (privacy preservation) and DEEP-SECURE (threat detection) but together they form a layered and holistic defense strategy.

The inclusion of real-time feedback loops in TRIDENT and DEEP-SECURE enhances system adaptability, allowing the frameworks to evolve with changing user behavior. Performance metrics such as execution time, scalability and precision show that all three systems can operate efficiently in real-world, high-volume platforms. The research demonstrates that hybrid techniques combining cryptographic models, clustering and neural networks yield better outcomes than standalone security methods. Ultimately, the integrated framework offers a viable solution for building secure, private and trustworthy environments in social media and other online platforms.

6.7. Summary

This chapter summarizes the key findings and discusses the outcomes of the three main contributions made throughout the research, aimed at improving trust, privacy and security in online social networks. In the first contribution, TRIDENT was developed to assess user trust and detect threats based on behavior patterns and content analysis. The model achieved strong classification accuracy, effectively identifying trusted, suspicious and malicious users. The integration of content authenticity mining, behavioral clustering and network trust evaluation proved essential in building a real-time trust assessment mechanism. A feedback loop further enhanced the system by updating trust scores dynamically, reflecting changes in user behavior. The second contribution, PRIVAFLOW, focused on enforcing privacy through attribute-based encryption and flow graph verification. This model introduced a flexible, context-aware access control mechanism that restricted data access to only those users who met specific attribute and relationship criteria. The model demonstrated high access control accuracy and successfully reduced unauthorized access rates. By incorporating privacy compatibility filtering, it ensured that even decrypted content was restricted according to the user's clearance level. The third contribution, DEEP-SECURE, introduced a robust intrusion detection framework powered by the KENSURE algorithm. This ensemble-based model used clustering, decision tree classification and kernelized neural networks to detect and verify threats with high accuracy and minimal false positives. It excelled in handling complex and evolving attack patterns while maintaining system performance under load. Collectively, the three frameworks form a comprehensive solution that addresses different layers of OSN security from user trust and behavior, to controlled data access, to intelligent threat detection. The research highlights the importance of multi-layered security strategies and the value of integrating different models to build resilient and scalable systems thereby opening pathways for future research in privacy-aware, secure online platforms.

CHAPTER-VII

CONCLUSION AND FUTURE ENHANCEMENTS

7.1. Introduction

Online Social Networks (OSNs) have rapidly evolved into essential digital platforms facilitating global communication, content sharing and social interaction. With billions of users actively engaging through posts, messages, multimedia and real-time conversations, OSNs have transformed the way people connect and consume information. Despite the numerous benefits these platforms offer, they have also emerged as vulnerable spaces prone to security breaches, privacy violations and misuse by malicious entities. The increasing reliance on OSNs for personal, professional and societal communication has amplified the need for robust systems that can safeguard user data, ensure content authenticity and detect harmful activities.

One of the major concerns in OSNs is the proliferation of misinformation, fake profiles, spam content, identity theft and targeted cyber-attacks. Traditional moderation techniques and reactive security models are often inadequate in addressing the fast-evolving nature of these threats. Many existing systems rely heavily on user reports or basic rule-based filters, which lack the sophistication to detect coordinated manipulation campaigns or deceptive user behavior. Moreover, as OSNs grow in scale and complexity, the need for intelligent frameworks that can operate efficiently in real-time environments becomes increasingly critical.

Another significant challenge lies in protecting user privacy while maintaining the functionality and openness of social platforms. Users frequently share personal details, multimedia and sensitive information without fully understanding the implications of data exposure. Standard privacy settings and access control mechanisms often fall short in offering granular and context-sensitive data protection. Unauthorized access, information leakage and misuse of personal data remain persistent issues, particularly in cloud-based OSN environments where data is distributed and accessed remotely.

In response to these pressing concerns, the present research proposes a comprehensive and layered approach to security and privacy in OSNs. The study is structured into three major contributions, each addressing a specific dimension of online safety. The first contribution introduces a trust-based framework that evaluates user credibility, content reliability and behavioral patterns using a structured social mining engine. It integrates semantic analysis, behavioral clustering and network trust modeling to identify suspicious or malicious activities. The second contribution focuses on strengthening privacy through an access control framework that combines attribute-based encryption with dynamic relationship analysis. This model ensures that data access decisions consider both the user's credentials and their trust-based relationship with the data owner, thus providing fine-grained and trust-aware privacy enforcement. The third and final contribution enhances threat detection through a multi-layered intrusion detection system. It employs clustering, decision trees and neural network techniques to perform a comprehensive analysis of user behavior, ensuring high detection accuracy while reducing false positives. The ensemble approach ensures that only users flagged across multiple validation stages are considered threats, thereby preserving legitimate user experiences.

Together, these contributions form a cohesive security architecture designed to address the multifaceted risks in OSNs. By combining trust evaluation, privacy preservation and intelligent threat detection, the research aims to build a resilient ecosystem that supports safe, secure and privacy-compliant interactions in social platforms. The study emphasizes practical implementation, scalability and adaptability, making it relevant for current and future challenges in the digital social landscape.

7.2. Summary of the research

The research presents a comprehensive, multi-phase security framework tailored for Online Social Networks (OSNs), focusing on enhancing user privacy, content authenticity and intrusion detection. The study is structured into three major contributions, each addressing a specific layer of OSN security: Contribution-I

(TRIDENT), Contribution-II (PRIVAFLOW with FISARA) and Contribution-III (DEEP-SECURE with KENSURE).

The first contribution, TRIDENT, establishes the foundation by introducing a multi-level trust-integrated model designed to monitor and evaluate users and their content within OSNs. The system comprises three critical analytical levels: Content Authenticity Mining, Behavioral Clustering and Network Trust Evaluation. At the heart of this framework is SOCMINE, a dedicated social mining engine that evaluates trust scores, user behavior and content reliability using a hybrid classification model based on Decision Trees and Support Vector machines. SOCMINE processes user-generated data in real time, performing behavioral pattern recognition, semantic content verification and clustering to identify threats. The system dynamically updates trust scores based on system feedback and user behavior, classifying users as trusted, suspicious, or malicious. A synthetically generated dataset of over 67,000 records simulates a realistic OSN environment for model validation. Results confirm TRIDENT's superior accuracy and detection rates over traditional models, offering scalable and efficient threat mitigation.

The second contribution shifts focus to privacy-preserving access control through the PRIVAFLOW framework. It integrates the Flow-Integrated Secure Attribute Retrieval Algorithm (FISARA), combining attribute-based encryption (ABE) and trust-aware flow verification. Unlike TRIDENT, which emphasizes user and content classification, PRIVAFLOW enforces fine-grained access control based on both user attributes and relational trust dynamics. PRIVAFLOW introduces a novel privacy rule mechanism, allowing data owners to define sensitivity levels for their content (low, medium, high). The system uses Enhanced ABE to encrypt data and applies a directed flow graph to validate access requests based on trust, confidence and interaction history. This dual-layer control ensures that only users with valid credentials and sufficient relational trust can access sensitive information. Moreover, the framework performs additional filtering based on keyword relevance, credential rules and privacy compatibility scores before decrypting and delivering content. It also incorporates audit logging, multi-agent validation and level-wise authorization to enhance reliability and transparency. Through comparative analysis,

PRIVAFLOW demonstrated higher precision and lower access latency than standard ABE models and TRIDENT, validating its efficiency in secure, privacy-centric data sharing.

The third and final contribution, DEEP-SECURE, introduces a sophisticated intrusion detection system built upon the KENSURE algorithm (Kernel-Enhanced Neural System for User Risk Evaluation). This ensemble model integrates three analytical modules: Clustering-Based Intrusion Detection, Decision Tree Classification and Kernelized Neural Network (KNN) Evaluation. Its objective is to detect malicious users with high precision while minimizing false positives. Initially, users are grouped through unsupervised clustering based on behavioral similarity. Outliers are flagged for further analysis. A decision tree then classifies users using entropy and Gini-based splits, followed by pruning to ensure generalization. Finally, a kernel-based neural network maps features into higher dimensions, allowing the system to capture non-linear relationships and refine classifications using Mahalanobis, Euclidean and Hamming distances. The ensemble nature of KENSURE mandates triple-verification before labeling a user as malicious. Only those flagged by all three modules undergo restriction or removal. Experimental validation demonstrated that DEEP-SECURE outperforms existing techniques such as SVM, ANN, CNN and AdaBoost in accuracy, recall and F1-score, proving its robustness for real-time OSN deployment. Together, these three contributions create a unified, end-to-end ecosystem for OSN security. TRIDENT excels in trust evaluation and threat detection, PRIVAFLOW strengthens privacy through dynamic access control and DEEP-SECURE introduces a highly accurate, layered detection strategy. Each framework builds upon the limitations of its predecessor, resulting in a holistic solution that ensures secure, trustworthy and privacy-preserving interactions in online social environments. The combined methodologies showcase a scalable approach adaptable to the evolving digital landscape, where user protection and data integrity are of utmost importance.

7.3. Conclusion of the research

The research undertaken through this multi-phase study presents a comprehensive security and privacy framework designed for Online Social

Networks (OSNs). Across three significant contributions, the work has addressed the core concerns of trust evaluation, data privacy enforcement and advanced threat detection in social platforms. The growing complexity of user interactions, the volume of user-generated content and the rising sophistication of malicious activities demand a holistic approach that goes beyond traditional access control or anomaly detection methods. This study fills that gap through the development of layered, intelligent models that work together to secure digital social ecosystems. The first phase, realized through the TRIDENT framework, introduced a trust-integrated social mining system capable of evaluating users and content based on behavior, semantic analysis and network interaction patterns. TRIDENT not only classifies users into trust-based categories but also provides a real-time, feedback-driven approach to continuously refine its trust scores and threat assessments. This creates a proactive security model that adapts to user behavior and contextual cues. Building upon this, the second phase introduced PRIVAFLOW, a structured framework designed to enforce privacy in OSNs by using a flow-based access control mechanism. PRIVAFLOW, through the integration of FISARA, enables fine-grained control of sensitive content using attribute-based encryption and flow graph verification. This ensures that user data is accessible only to those who satisfy both policy rules and trust relationship thresholds. The mechanism avoids generic or static privacy settings, providing a more dynamic and secure way to handle personal information in a cloud-based social environment. The final phase, DEEP-SECURE, focused on enhancing the precision of intrusion detection through the KENSURE algorithm. This model employs an ensemble structure combining clustering, decision trees and kernel-based neural networks to identify high-risk users. Unlike single-layer models, DEEP-SECURE performs multi-stage validation to minimize false positives and increase threat detection accuracy. It provides a layered, adaptive mechanism that operates on diverse behavioral indicators and complex user activity data.

Together, these three contributions form a unified and scalable solution that responds to the evolving needs of social platforms. Each phase targets a different dimension of digital security—be it evaluating user trust, enforcing data confidentiality, or detecting threats with higher accuracy. The combination of these models results in a more secure, privacy-preserving and reliable environment for users to engage and share content. The results from simulations and comparative evaluations clearly demonstrate the efficiency, accuracy and robustness of the proposed methods, offering meaningful contributions to the field of OSN security.

7.4. Future enhancements

Although the proposed frameworks TRIDENT, PRIVAFLOW and DEEP-SECURE have demonstrated significant advancements in trust analysis, privacy protection and threat detection, there remain several opportunities to extend and refine these systems. Future enhancements can focus on both technical improvements and practical adaptations for broader deployment in dynamic social platforms. One of the primary areas for improvement lies in real-time scalability. While the current models have been tested on large-scale datasets, integration into live OSN environments with millions of active users will require optimization for speed and resource efficiency. Stream-based data handling mechanisms and distributed computing frameworks can be introduced to process user activities, content analysis and trust evaluations without latency.

Another direction for future work is enhancing explainability and user transparency. As security models become more complex, users and administrators alike must understand the reasoning behind access denials, trust scores, or threat classifications. Introducing interpretable decision paths, audit trails and user-facing feedback mechanisms can promote trust in the system and ensure compliance with privacy regulations. From a technical standpoint, the models can be extended to incorporate deep contextual understanding of multimedia content. Presently, much of the content analysis focuses on textual data and metadata. Integrating computer vision techniques for image and video content validation would enhance the system's ability to detect visual misinformation or malicious media. Additionally, sentiment analysis, linguistic deception cues and temporal interaction modeling could offer deeper behavioral insights. In the realm of access control, PRIVAFLOW's attribute and flow-based policy verification can be expanded by integrating blockchain-based identity and consent mechanisms. This would allow users to have greater ownership over their data and verify access permissions through decentralized ledgers. Furthermore, adaptive access policies that learn and evolve with user preferences can provide a more personalized privacy experience.

Another promising area for enhancement is cross-platform threat intelligence. Social media users often engage across multiple platforms and malicious actors tend to exploit these interconnections. Establishing secure data exchange mechanisms between different OSN systems could enable shared detection of coordinated attacks or impersonation efforts, thereby improving early warning systems. In conclusion, while the current research lays a solid foundation for OSN security and privacy, its future potential lies in greater adaptability, broader content awareness, user-centric design and ethical foresight. As digital interactions continue to expand in scale and complexity, these enhancements will help the proposed frameworks remain relevant and resilient in securing the next generation of online social platforms.

www.ingramcontent.com/pod-product-compliance
Lightning Source LLC
LaVergne TN
LVHW010723061126
851857LV00014B/1316

* 9 7 9 8 2 5 6 2 5 8 0 2 3 *